FLORAL CAKE DECORATING

FLORAL CAKE DECORATING

NORMA DUNN

Souvenir Press

Published by Gregory's Publishing Company
a division of Universal Press Pty Ltd
64 Talavera Road, Macquarie Park, New South Wales, 2113, Australia

First published 1977
First British Edition
published 1983 by Souvenir Press Ltd
43 Great Russell Street, London WC1B 3PA

ISBN 0 285 62581 0

Designed by Jill Day

Typeset by Auckland Typographical Services Ltd., Auckland
Printed by Colourwork Press Pte Ltd
21 Mandai Estate, Singapore 2572

Cover: Photograph shows the work of one of Norma Dunn's star pupils, Judy Messing, of
Turramurra, New South Wales. She made the cream hexagonal birthday cake specially for this
book cover, and decorated it with a spray of pink tiger lilies, snowdrops and eriostemon. *The cake
was awarded 1st prize in the Birthday Cake section at the 1979 Royal Easter Show.*

Contents

Introduction

I have much pleasure presenting this cake decorating book, with detailed instructions accompanying every exercise. Beautiful photographs in black and white show how to make every flower, step by step, giving even the beginner the confidence to attempt any flower.

Gone are the days when cake decorating was regarded as a kitchen hobby. My love of cake decorating, particularly making flowers in sugar, has led me to spend years experimenting to improve and perfect new methods. They have been tried and proved by my pupils' successes. I have always striven to make a flower quickly, efficiently and as lifelike as possible.

Cake decorating and making flowers such as those shown here can become a fascinating hobby—even a paying one. Beautifully made flowers will always find a ready market. It is an art in which every decorator can exercise skill and initiative.

Proceed carefully. When you have mastered one flower and can make it well, try another and you will experience a great sense of achievement. Do not attempt too many flowers at once. It is better to make a few flowers beautifully than none really well. Become aware of flowers around you—study them, experiment and you could create yet another flower. For the keen decorator, this field of cake decorating is endless.

I have included color plates of lovely moulded sprays of flowers. You will also find, in the second half of the book, photos of a selection of decorated cakes. They will help you in arranging flowers and designing cakes for every occasion. The designs are all simple and will be appreciated by every cake decorator.

I trust you will have many years of pleasure from this book but, remember, the ingredients for success are patience, practice and perseverance.

Norma Dunn
Sydney, 1978

Requirements
for Successful
Flower Making

All your equipment for making flowers should be kept on a tray, so it may be put away when not in use and brought out when required. Everything is then there, ready for you to start.

Following is the simple equipment I use when moulding flowers.

1. Modelling stick. This cannot be bought in any shop. I found when I started moulding flowers many years ago I had to use my own initiative and "invent" certain "instruments" to create exactly what I wanted. I made my modelling stick from a cheap paint brush handle. Buy the smallest size, OO, cut off the handle just above the brush and, using fine sandpaper, round the end to a nice smooth finish, and shape the other end to a gentle point, but don't have it sharp. It is important to have the modelling stick pointed end nice and fine for a length of 2.5 cm (1 inch). Unless it is fine, you will not be able to make beautiful flowers. A thickened "stem" will not fit into the "throat" of a small flower. The rounded end is used to shape flowers such as gum nuts and lily-of-the-valley.

2. Small scissors. Invest in a good pair of scissors. Use straight or curved, the shaft part being as short and fine as possible so you can work close to the flower when cutting.

3. Knife. A really good knife is very important so you can cut quickly and efficiently. Forget the kitchen knife and buy a scalpel from a chemist. Stainless steel is better than chrome.

4. Hair curler pin. On one side there is a slight ridge, and I use that when required to "vein" a petal to make the flower look more realistic. A packet of hair curler pins may be bought in a chain store.

5. Rolling pin. Obviously a normal rolling pin cannot be used for rolling out tiny pieces of modelling paste. I use an ordinary meat skewer. Cut off the point, smooth with fine sandpaper and it is ready for use.

6. Paint brushes. Your paint brushes are a very important part of your equipment, so always spend a little more and buy good quality sable hair brushes. They are not cheap, but will last you indefinitely if you treat them with care. Rinse in cold water after use and dry flat – never stand brush on hairs to dry, or they will dry bent. On no account use cheap brushes – the hairs fall out and you will not be able to paint flowers efficiently. You will need several, a No. 0 or a No. OO, a No. 3 and a No. 5. It is a good idea to have two or three of the larger brushes – when painting with several colors, it saves time washing brushes.

7. Tweezers. An essential item for adding stamens to flowers, and sprays to an arrangement. I prefer tweezers with a slanted point. Whether slanted or pointed is not important, so long as you can handle them.

8. Wire scissors. Do not use your flower scissors for cutting wire

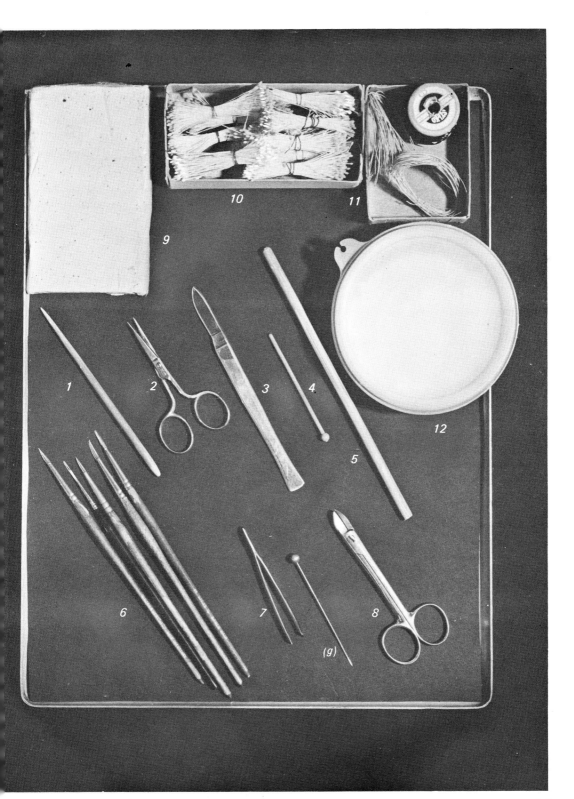

11

or you will ruin the cutting edge. Have a special pair of scissors for the purpose.

9. Foundation clay. Often used in dried flower arrangements, but I use it when making small flowers. When completing a flower, insert wire into clay and leave to dry. You could also use a board with nail holes 5 cm (2 inches) apart.

10. Stamens. Keep a box on your tray containing several bundles of colored, preferably fine tipped, stamens.

11. Wire. This is essential for wiring flowers. Fine wire is used for all small flowers and a heavier one for flowers which require a stronger support, such as daffodil, daisy and rose. A good general rule to follow is to use wire as fine as possible, and yet strong enough to support the flower you are making, to give a dainty appearance. Two cake decorators could use a different wire when making the same flower. It would depend on how finely you mould. You can buy wire from shops selling cake-decorating supplies. If you can't buy it from a shop, you might be able to approach a firm which manufactures wire and buy a reel, which you could share between several decorators. Fuse wire can be used for some small flowers, but you must be prepared to experiment to find the wire to suit you.

12. Cornflour. Keep a small bowl of cornflour, preferably one with a lid, on your tray. You will require it to dust your fingers when moulding.

The following items are also required when moulding, arranging or painting flowers:

(a) **Modelling board.** A laminex-covered board about 30 x 20 cm (12 x 8 inches) is a good size, and is required for rolling out and cutting.

(b) **Icing sugar.** Keep a special bowl for pure icing sugar, which should be freshly sieved every time you mould. A good sized bowl is 7 cm deep (2¾ inches) and 18 cm (7 inches) across the top. That will allow you to work your paste over the bowl with ease.

(c) A small bowl of water for dipping wires and attaching petals.

(d) **Alfoil.** Alfoil is far superior to waxed paper, and I use it for assembling large flowers such as roses and frangipani, shaping leaves and storing flowers.

(e) **Food colors.** I use liquid food colors for painting flowers. Start with basic colors – blue, burgundy red, green, yellow, violet and brown.

(f) **Painting tray.** If you are mixing your colors on a saucer and then washing them off afterwards, buy a painting tray with about ten sections, and use for mixing colors. The liquid will dry, but the color will remain and may be used again with a damp brush.

(g) **Darning needle or hat pin.** (Illustrated) This is not used in making flowers, but is indispensable when arranging flowers on a cake. A small hole is first pierced into the icing, and then using tweezers, flower sprays are inserted.

Methods 2
Employed in
Moulding Flowers

There are three methods I employ in moulding flowers—finger-shaping, hollowing and freehand cutting. Every flower in this book is made using at least one of those methods, so it is important before attempting any flowers to understand and master the three techniques.

1. Finger-shaping. Just what is meant by finger-shaping? The words themselves are self-explanatory – it is simply creating a shape with the fingers. So many flowers require finger-shaping of petals, such as roses, mock orange blossom, poppy, just to mention a few, that it is important to master the correct finger-shaping of a petal.

If you are able to obtain a rose, then take several various-sized petals, study them and use them as a guide. If not, follow these instructions carefully. The consistency of your modelling paste must be soft enough to enable you to shape the petal, yet firm enough so that the completed petal will hold its shape when attached to a flower, or set aside to dry.

Take a small quantity of paste and knead in a little pure sifted icing sugar until the correct consistency is obtained. Only after practice and experience will you be able to determine what "correct" is. Remember a pea-sized piece of paste can be thinned out with the tips of the fingers to paper thickness about the size of a 20 cent piece. That will give you some idea just how much paste will be required to mould a petal.

Keep the tips of the fingers lightly dusted with cornflour and you should not experience any difficulty with the icing sticking. Never allow a build up of icing to occur on the fingers. Wash the hands, dry thoroughly and redust fingers with cornflour.

Start with a piece of paste about the size of a pea. If you find you can't manage such a small piece, then use a larger piece. Remember the size will determine the size of the petal, and in turn the size of the flower. Now press the piece of paste between the thumb and forefinger of the left hand, and point the base of the petal with the thumb and forefinger of the right hand. The shape of the petal is now there. All that is required is to thin it. Using the tips of the fingers of both hands, start at the base of the petal (the point), and work around the petal, thinning as finely as possible towards the edge.

When you have mastered the shaping of the petal, the next step is to be able to curl the petal on the edges to give an attractive appearance to the flower. You can do that in one of two ways, either "palm" the petal, or shape it over the thumb. "Palming" the petal will cup it and give a soft curl to the edge, but it must be finely moulded. Simply cup the hand, dust with a little cornflour, and place the petal in the palm of the hand. Place the thumb firmly but gently on the petal, and with the forefinger, curl petal edges back. Do not push hard or you will get a "pushed-in thumb" look to the petal.

The second way, place the petal over the cushion part of the thumb, and with the fingers curl petal edges back. Sometimes the petal is shaped and attached to the flower, and then the petals curled with the fingers. An example would be a medium rose.

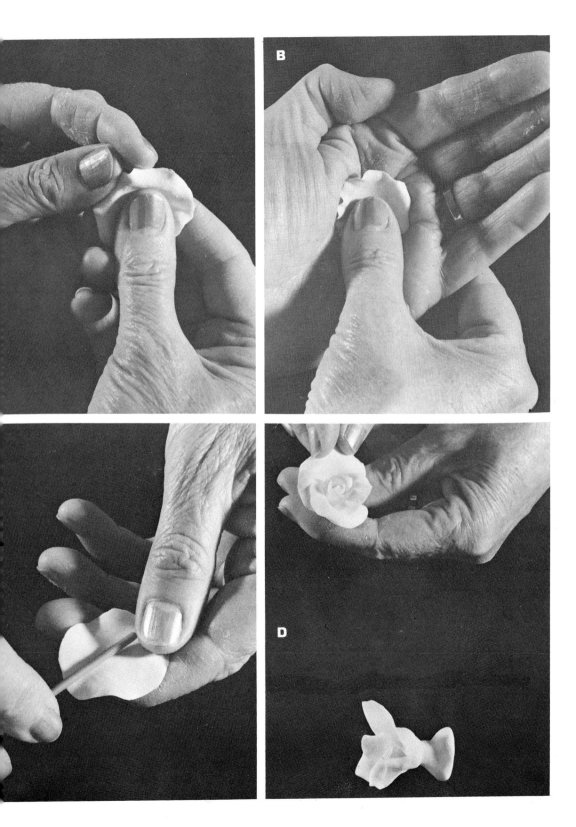

When you feel you have reached a degree of efficiency in first, shaping and second, curling the petals, then you are ready to tackle some of the flowers where finger-shaping is required. You could try Dainty Bess rose, full-blown rose and Cecil Brunner rose. In some exercises reference is made to "fluting" or "veining" a petal. It is just a little extra shaping given to a petal after it is made, to make it even more realistic. To "flute" a petal, simply place the modelling stick behind a petal edge, and pinch with the fingers. As you move it around the petal edge, repeat to give more curl to the petal. To "vein" a petal, use item 4 in "Requirements for successful flower making". It is rolled across a petal, and leaves a veining on the petal. If you are a beginner, then there is no need to worry about it.

2. Hollowing. I use this method to make many small flowers such as bouvardia, snowdrops or lilac, and larger flowers such as Christmas bells, freesias and daisies, just to mention a few.

Take a pea-sized piece of paste, roll between fingers to about 10 mm (½ inch) long, and flatten top with forefinger.

It doesn't matter if you start with a larger ball. The main thing is to master the hollowing, then you will find you will gradually reduce the size of the piece of paste until you can manage a tiny ball.

Now insert modelling stick (the pointed end is always used for hollowing tiny flowers, unless the exercise states otherwise) and hollow finely. Don't just insert the modelling stick and move it in a circular motion. That won't achieve a fine edge. Hold the shape with the thumb and the first two fingers of the left hand, and resting it on the forefinger, insert modelling stick and roll anti-clockwise, and at the same time swivel the piece of paste clockwise, and firmly work the sides out until they are nice and fine. If necessary, dust finger with cornflour.

Practise, using small balls of paste until you have mastered the technique, then you will find it so much easier when you attempt to make flowers using this method. Sometimes in an exercise reference will be made to "thin". It is just an extension of hollowing a flower. You might find after hollowing and cutting the petals they could be finer. Then, using the modelling stick, roll it around the petals once again to complete the shaping. In some flowers such as the daisy and flannel flower, the hollowing is not fine to start with, and the petals are "thinned" after they have been cut and shaped.

3. Freehand cutting. Most flowers are made using the first two methods. However, when rolling and cutting is necessary, you will find freehand cutting will give you a more natural flower or leaf. Of course, if you find you can't manage, then you will have to cut a pattern. The water-lily and orchid are two flowers where freehand cutting is adopted.

Dust board lightly with cornflour, and roll out as finely as possible just sufficient paste to do the job, moving the paste around to make sure it has not stuck. Using a scalpel, cut out cleanly. Always see the blade of your knife is perfectly clean and free from any grains of dried paste, to ensure a smooth, clean cut.

Hollowing out a small flower with modelling stick. Fern is made with a piping bag and royal icing.

Petals sometimes need thinning after cutting and shaping. See under (1) finger-shaping.

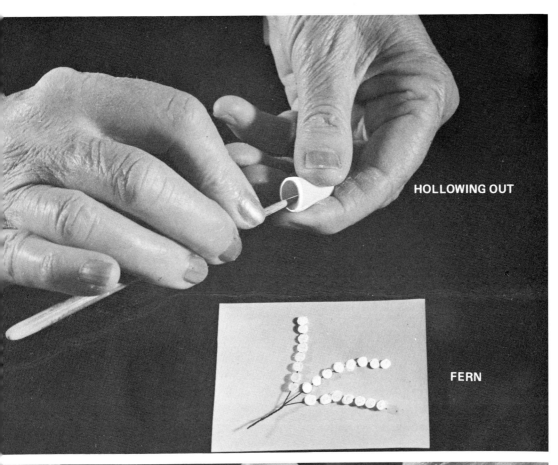

HOLLOWING OUT

FERN

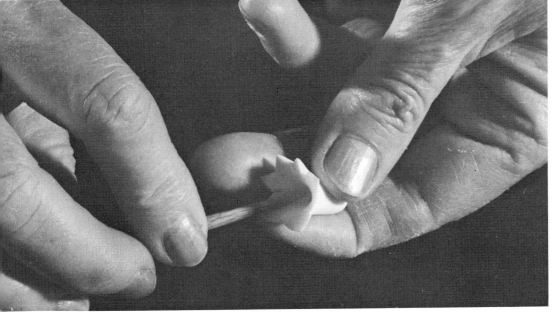

Hints for the Decorator 3

1. Buy narrow white satin ribbon by the roll, it is far more economical. It may be tinted the exact color you require to match your cake covering or flowers. Simply add a few drops of food coloring to a small jar of water. Immerse the ribbon completely, withdraw and run it firmly through a piece of towelling several times to remove moisture. If done correctly it should not be streaked. Leave to dry, and iron, or iron dry. The dye will keep almost indefinitely.

2. Buy the narrowest ribbon — 5 mm width.

3. Cut ribbon in half, it will go farther and will look daintier on a cake.

4. If you wish to make satin ribbon stand up when looped, lie ribbon flat on towel, lightly spray with hair spray and iron on a cool setting.

5. Don't waste wire, cut only the length required. You will find 3.5 to 4 cm (1¼ to 1½ inches) is quite long enough for small flowers. When twisted together the finished spray will be longer. For a top posy, 8 to 10 cm (3 to 4 inches) is long enough.

6. If for any reason a wire needs to be lengthened for an arrangement, simply twist a short length to the end — it will not be seen.

7. Use fuse wire for gum nuts, wattle, holly berries and heather.

8. Wire must always be dipped in water to attach to flower. Remember, if a flower tapers down the wire, wire must be moistened to that depth.

9. Use egg white to attach a leaf on to a wire. When it dries, leaf will set firmly, but handle carefully. Water is not successful.

10. Always put a small hook on the end of your wire, making sure it is well pressed in when making tiny flowers, so it will not tear the throat of the flower when inserted. There is no need to hook wire when making tiny buds.

11. Any flowers assembled on alfoil, such as roses, frangipani, or similar, leave on the alfoil and pack away, as it will protect them until required. They can be wired any time. If wiring before storing, place the stem through the alfoil, and then pack.

12. Always make sure your box containing stored flowers is deep enough. Remember petals are easily broken if care is not taken in handling.

13. Always store flowers in a dry place.

14. Silica-gel crystals are excellent for keeping flowers dry. Place some crystals in cupped alfoil in the box. Silica-gel may be bought from a chemist. Crystals are a deep blue/violet when dry. As soon as they have absorbed moisture they change to pink. To return them to their original color, spread on a tray and place in the oven at 125deg.C (250deg.F) – no hotter or you will burn them. As soon as they have returned to blue they may be used again.

15. If you have made a lot of petals in a patty pan and you are waiting for them to dry to assemble, sprinkle silica-gel crystals in each compartment and they will dry very quickly.

16. When painting flowers, use color sparingly. Try on a spare petal first.

17. Use red food powder when moulding red roses, poinsettia, waratah, Christmas decorations, and similar, and touch up with liquid food coloring when flower is completed. If you mould in white, the area to be colored is too great – petals could be softened in the painting and if any white is missed, it will show.

18. Use a small tipped green stamen for lily-of-the-valley flowers instead of wire.

19. Tiny pieces of cut stamen stem are used in small flowers where stamens are not suitable. It gives a very dainty appearance to the flower. The pieces are tipped in color.

20. I use a large brush for dusting the top of the cake after arranging a flower spray. Flowers will not be damaged and cake covering will not be smudged.

21. Stamens are becoming increasingly difficult to buy, particularly fine tipped ones. DO NOT throw away the portion remaining after you have cut the stamen from either end of the bundle. To make your own place about 1 teaspoon of egg white in a saucer and, in another, a little gelatine. Take a stem and dip either end (only the tip), first in egg white then in gelatine and place on a sheet of waxed paper to set. Do not try to dip the bundle all at once as each one must be done separately to achieve a beautiful fine-tipped stamen. When dry, gather into a bundle, securing with a piece of wire in the centre, and they are ready for use. Using a fine brush, tip in color.

22. Use a No. 0 or No. 00 paint brush for fine tipping, a No. 3 for general painting and a No. 5 for petals, or similar when you have a larger area to paint. If you do a lot of cake decorating, buy two each of No. 3 and No. 5.

23. Cut your stamens from the bundle, not the bundle from the stamens. In other words, gather the number of stamens required by the head, hold firmly, and cut from the bundle. Still holding them, curve over the fingers for a realistic appearance, and with tweezers insert directly into the flower. If making tiny flowers, put the flower down to cut the stamens. After cutting stamens, pick up flower and hold firmly between the forefinger and the next finger,

(a)

LOOPING RIBBON

(b)

Cut ribbon in half for a dainty appearance and loop as shown in diagrams (a). Fold a short length of wire in half and twist firmly around base. Do not wind wire around ribbon as shown in (b) as it creates bulk around the base.

just at the base of the flower, the stamens being held with the thumb and forefinger. Try it, it is so much easier than chasing stamens all over the table, as so many decorators do.

24. Do not use green straight from the bottle for painting leaves, or similar, mix with a little brown and yellow.

25. When making flowers where centres have to be made on wire and allowed to dry, such as sweet pea, daisy or Cecil Brunner rose, make several dozen. They will keep and will be ready to complete when required.

26. A few hints on icing sugar:
(a) Use only pure icing sugar.
(b) Feel icing sugar before you buy. Never buy icing sugar which feels hard or lumpy.

22

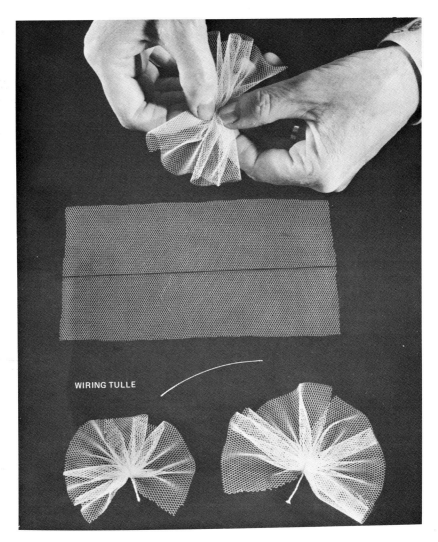

Cut a piece of tulle about 15 cm (6 inches) long and 8 to 10 cm (3 to 4 inches) deep, depending on the height of your arrangement. Pleat tulle with fingers as shown in diagram ar twist a piece of wir firmly around the centre. Using finger fan it out.

WIRING TULLE

(c) Icing sugar may be kept in the refrigerator to prevent it going hard.

(d) Keep a fine sieve for cake decorating only, also mixing spoons.

LOOPING RIBBON

Cut ribbon in half for a dainty appearance and loop as shown in diagram (a). Fold a short length of wire in half and twist firmly around base. Do not wind wire around ribbon as shown in (b) as it creates bulk around the base.

WIRING TULLE

Cut a piece of tulle about 15 cm (6 inches) long and 8 to 10 cm (3 to 4 inches) in depth depending on the height of your arrangement. Pleat tulle with fingers as shown in diagram and twist a piece of wire firmly around the centre. Using fingers, fan out.

23

Flower
Exercises

If you have read carefully the previous chapters and familiarised yourself thoroughly with chapters 2 and 3, then you are ready to begin moulding.

Before starting, see that you are comfortable, and everything is on hand to save getting up and down for something forgotten. Set up your tray on a table covered with a sheet of plastic. You will find the following helpful.

(a) Wear an apron.

(b) Have a bowl of freshly sieved icing sugar on hand.

(c) A damp cloth to wipe your hands. Remember, do not allow a build up of icing to occur on the tips of your fingers. The slightest mark on your petals will show.

(d) Work up a small quantity of modelling paste with icing sugar to the required consistency, leaving the balance in a covered container. You will need a soft consistency for moulding petals finely, and a firmer consistency for small flowers. If the consistency is not firm enough when making small flowers, you will not have control over the piece of paste and it will not hold its shape. Place modelling paste in a small plastic bag and leave the top open for easy access. Place on your lap and cover with hand towel. Don't forget modelling paste will become hard if left exposed to the air.

To save constant repetition throughout the exercises, do not forget to observe the following points:

1. Hook wires when making small flowers, except for buds, and moisten to attach – refer Chapter 3 "Hints for the Decorator", paragraphs 8 and 10.

2. When making flowers such as Cecil Brunner rose and medium rose, always brush a little water on base of each petal to attach to flower. This applies to any flower where petals are positioned as they are made. Royal icing is used only to assemble the flowers after petals are made and allowed to dry, e.g. full blown rose, mock orange blossom, briar rose or similar.

HOLLY LEAVES AND BERRIES

Holly leaves and berries make a simple yet colorful decoration for a Christmas cake, and are very simple for the beginner to manage.
Leaves. Mould in pale green and try to cut the leaves freehand. If you feel you are unable to do this, cut a pattern. Roll out a small quantity of modelling paste as finely as practicable on a board lightly dusted with cornflour, place pattern in position and, using a scalpel, carefully cut out leaf. Notice in the diagram how I have continued the cut into the icing away from each curve. That will give you a nice clean edge. Lightly vein leaf with scalpel, being careful not to cut through the leaf. Pick up and repoint each tip if necessary with thumb and forefinger, and place on alfoil to dry.

When dry, paint with a mixture of brown, green and yellow to give a nice deep color. This is one case where bright colors are permissible. In the exercise I have displayed some real leaves and berries and you will notice there is no set number of curves to either side of

From top to bottom: Holly, berry and leaf, wattle, gum nuts.

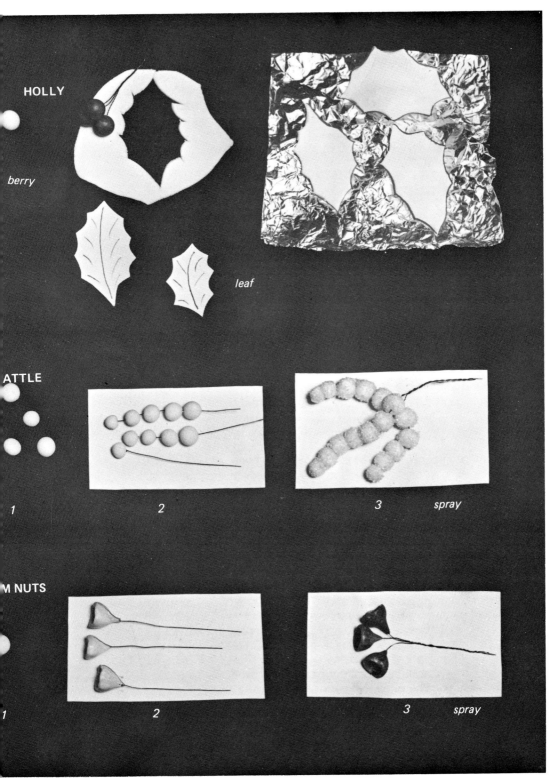

HOLLY

berry

leaf

ATTLE

1   2   3   spray

M NUTS

1   2   3   spray

27

the leaf. As the leaves get nearer the tip of the spray there is very little shaping.

Berries. Mould with a little scarlet food coloring in the paste. You will find it a lot easier to paint afterwards. Roll small balls of paste in palm of hand to form berry shape, and allow them to roll directly from the palm of your hand on to the board. Berries look very nice wired, and it dispenses with the use of royal icing to attach to cake. Hook small lengths of fine wire, moisten end and insert into each berry shortly after making. When dry, twist two or three together to form a spray and, holding by the wire, paint berries scarlet. Wire directly into cake at the base of several leaves.

DAINTY BESS ROSE

This beautiful rose is used widely by cake decorators. It always looks lovely on a wedding cake and combines with a wide variety of flowers to make an attractive decoration.

Before starting to make the flower, cut some alfoil squares 6 cm (2½ inches) on which to assemble the flowers.

1. Finger-shape five petals, and as each one is made, place in patty pan to set. The size of the piece of paste will determine the size of the petal, and in turn, the size of the flower. Make flowers in varying sizes so you will have a choice when·making an arrangement.

2. To assemble the flower. Place a square of alfoil on the palm of your left hand and with a No. 5 tube, squeeze just sufficient royal icing into the centre to position the five petals, each petal overlapping the previous petal slightly. Place over patty pan, and with fingers, ease in.

3. With a No. 5 tube, pipe a star into the centre, drawing to a point. Make sure your royal icing is firm, otherwise stamens will flop. Holding stamens by the head, cut just sufficient to give the flower an attractive appearance. Bend over finger, and with tweezers, insert one at a time around the centre. You will need ten to sixteen fine tipped stamens, depending on the size of the flower, about 20mm (⅝ inch) long. DO NOT clump a lot of stamens into the centre all at once, or have them too short. That makes for a most unattractive flower.

Note. This flower may be wired and so give height to an arrangement. Mould calyx in pale green as for hyacinth. After cutting to a point, "thin", insert wire down through the centre, turn flower carefully upside down, moisten inside of calyx and place on back of flower. Firmly position and leave to dry. Paint flowers a delicate shade of pink on the backs of the petals, and if petals are finely moulded, the color will show through.

The following method of making the flower is only for the more experienced decorator, as the flower may be assembled as the petals are made. The petals must be finely moulded and when completed firm enough to hold their shape. Ease a square of alfoil into a patty pan, finger-shape the first petal and place in alfoil cup.

Alfoil is used as a base for moulding these three flowers: (top) Dainty Bess rose, showing wired flower, bud, and leaves. (bottom) mock orange blossom, and Christmas rose and bud.

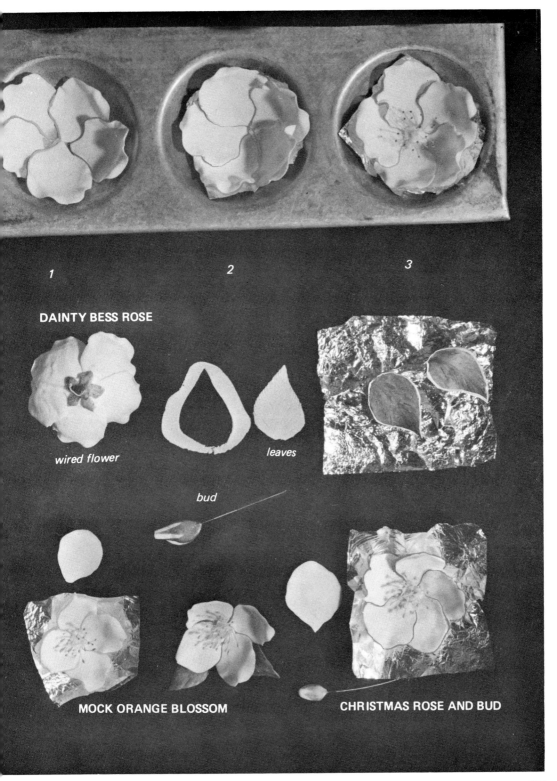

DAINTY BESS ROSE

wired flower

leaves

bud

MOCK ORANGE BLOSSOM

CHRISTMAS ROSE AND BUD

1   2   3

Finger-shape the remaining four petals, and as each petal is completed, moisten **the back of the base of petal only** and position,
each petal slightly overlapping the previous petal. Leave to completely dry, and then add the stamens. The flower will slip off the
alfoil easily and cleanly. Only a touch of moisture is necessary. DO
NOT saturate petals and when attaching, firmly position with
finger.

Bud. Mould bud as for Cecil Brunner rose and paint a calyx around
bud when dry.

Rose leaf. Leaf may be finger-shaped finely, marked with scalpel
and left to dry. You will find that method a lot quicker. However,
modelling paste may be rolled out in pale green and either freehand
cut or use a pattern. Cut out leaf, mark and vein, and for an extra
realistic touch, using scalpel finely nick edge of leaf. Place on alfoil
to dry, then paint. When painting, do not use green straight from
the bottle. Blend with a little brown and yellow.

MOCK ORANGE BLOSSOM

This dainty flower is ideal when an all-white cake is requested. It has
four petals and a mass of yellow stamens in the centre, the flower
rather open in appearance. Any small white flowers would be suitable to arrange with mock orange blossom, such as hyacinths or
lily-of-the-valley.

Finger-shape four petals a little smaller than those of the Dainty
Bess rose, and when dry assemble in the same way on a small
square of alfoil. Squeeze a No. 5 star into the centre and draw to a
point. Insert yellow-tipped stamens with tweezers around the
centre. The flower may be wired.

POINSETTIA

Here is yet another simple flower for you to make combining freehand cutting and hollowing methods. This lovely flower is suitable
not only for a Christmas decoration, but looks wonderful on a boy's
cake.

1. First make the centre and mould in pale green. Using very tiny
balls of modelling paste, hollow about twelve pieces (the first two
stages of the bouvardia) allowing each one to drop straight into a
box and leave to completely dry. Brush the rim with red food coloring or egg white, and dip in sieved raspberry jelly crystals. To give a
more realistic touch to the centre, very tiny pieces of yellow modelling paste are attached to one side of the centre pieces near the top
after centres are completely dry (using just a touch of moisture to
hold) and marked across the top with your scalpel.

2. It is easier to mould this stage in color by using a little red
powder in the paste, or liquid food coloring. Try to cut your petals
freehand, it will give a far more natural appearance than using a
pattern. Cut about twenty, varying in size from 1 cm to 4 cm (1/2
inch to 1 1/2 inches), it will depend on their size and how you arrange

Various stages in
making poinsettia and
leaf, and arum lily.
(Instructions pages
30 and 32.)

30

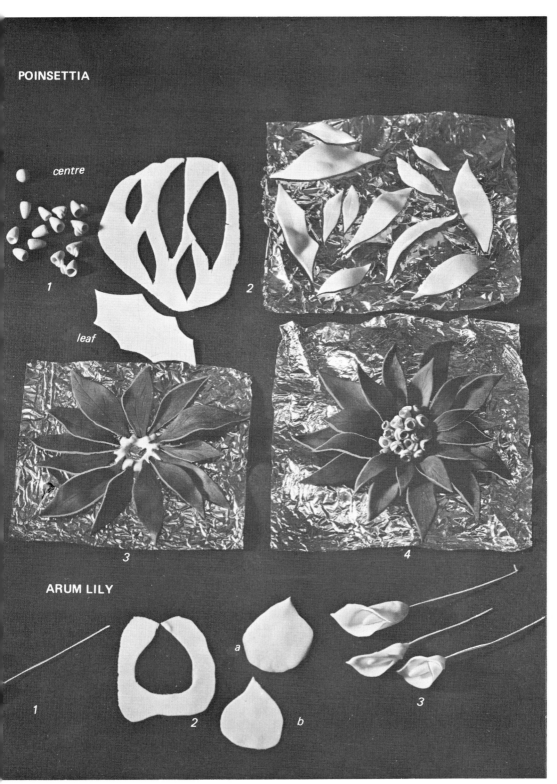

POINSETTIA

centre

leaf

1

2

3

4

ARUM LILY

1

2

a

b

3

them. Roll out sufficient modelling paste finely to cut two or three petals at a time. The amount you roll out will depend on how quickly you can cut and vein each petal. The modelling paste will dry and set quickly once it has been rolled finely, so you will find it better to roll just sufficient paste for you to handle. Mark and vein each petal carefully with your scalpel and place on alfoil as shown in diagram. When completely dry paint petals, but don't get flower too dark. Brush a little brown through the red while petals are still wet.

3. To assemble flower. Take a square of alfoil sufficiently large to assemble the flower, squeeze a circle of royal icing into the centre and arrange the petals as shown.

4. Finally add centre pieces using tweezers and leave to dry. If you wish to raise a petal slightly, place a small piece of rolled alfoil behind petal, leave to set and then remove alfoil with tweezers.

Leaf. Cut out leaf shape in pale green modelling paste, freehand if possible, mark and vein and place on alfoil to dry. Paint with a mixture of brown, green and yellow, brushing a little red along the centre vein towards the base of the leaf. See illustration page 31.
Note. This flower can look very flat on a cake, but it can be wired in the same manner as described for Dainty Bess rose.

ARUM LILY

The Arum lily is a large flower, but may be made on a smaller scale, and is suitable for a confirmation cake.

1. Mould the centre in yellow by rolling a small ball of paste to shape as shown, insert wire up through the base, firm with fingers and leave to dry. When dry, coat with crystals in the same manner as for wattle (page 33), keeping base free of crystals to allow for application of petal.

2. When the centre has dried, make and attach the outside petal. Either (a) finger-shape petal or (b) roll out paste finely and cut freehand or from a pattern.

3. Apply petal to base of centre with a little moisture, allowing the petal to lap slightly, and with tips of fingers, curl back top edge softly and point petal tip.
When painting, brush a soft shading of green towards the base on the outside of the flower. **Note** – The lily may be painted in pink or yellow. Flowers are wired singly into an arrangement.

CHRISTMAS ROSE

The Christmas rose (Helleborus niger) is white, saucer-shaped with golden stamens. It has five smooth-edged petals, slightly cup-shaped, with just a touch of green around the base. The flowers are large but may be scaled down for cake decoration.

1. Finger shape five smooth-edged petals, slightly cup either in palm of hand or over thumb. Leave to dry.

2. Assemble in the same way as the Dainty Bess rose, adding tiny golden-tipped stamens around the centre.

Bud. Mould bud shape as shown, paint calyx around base. This rose can also be wired. See Dainty Bess rose.
Leaves. Roll out paste in green, cut leaves to shape, leave to dry, then paint.

WATTLE

Here is another very simple exercise for you. Wattle can be made to look dainty, and is very effective when arranged in a spray of wildflowers, giving a softening effect to the bright colors of some of our Australian wildflowers such as the waratah and Christmas bell.

1. Mould in yellow and make small balls in varying sizes in the same manner as you did for holly berries.

2. After making about a dozen, insert a length of hooked fine wire into the first tiny ball, but don't push it through. Now thread small balls on to the wire just as though you were threading beads, varying the numbers on each wire and placing smaller ones towards the tip.

3. When completely dry, twist two or three wires to form a spray and, holding by the wire, lightly brush over flowers with a little egg white, then dust either with colored castor sugar or sieved lemon jelly crystals to give a lovely "powder" look to the spray, and place on waxed paper to dry. **Note.** Do not try to hasten the process and dip spray directly into egg white, or you will find after dipping into crystals they will absorb surplus egg white, sugar grains will soften and the whole appearance will be ruined.
To color castor sugar, simply place a little in a saucer, add a drop of yellow food coloring and blend through. Jelly crystals are ready for use after sieving.

GUM NUTS

Sprays of gum nuts are also very effective when included in a wildflower arrangement. The rounded end of the modelling stick is used for this simple exercise.

1 and 2. The gum nuts may be moulded in either white or yellow paste and painted when dry. Using a small pea size piece of paste, mould over rounded end of modelling stick, insert fine wire down through the centre and firm at base with fingers. Leave to dry.

3. Twist to form small sprays, hold by wire and paint with brown food coloring. You may need two coats but don't get them too dark.

MEDIUM ROSE

The rose, with soft and delicate tonings of pinks, cream to yellow or apricot, is ideally suited to cake decoration. Even a red rose is sometimes called for on a cake such as a ruby wedding or a mother's day cake. If you are able to mould a beautiful rose, then you are equipped to decorate any cake for any occasion. An arrangement of roses and leaves alone will make a perfect spray, while they combine admirably with any number of small flowers and even larger flowers such as fuchsia or daisies.

As there are several types of roses mentioned in this book, I have called this particular rose "medium rose" simply because it is in a medium stage of growth. I recommend you practise this flower and perfect it.

1. To make the centre, take a large ball of modelling paste about the size of a walnut and with fingers roll to form a log shape. The size of the ball of paste will determine the size of the flower. Keeping one side untouched, thin out opposite side (the long side) with fingers to a fine edge. **Note** – the thick part forms the base, the fine edge the top of the rolled centre.

2. Now roll the edge (shaded) in towards the centre, running thumb along the edge to form a fine point. Hold the fingers of the left hand near the top as you roll to form the centre with the right hand, keeping a nice fine point.

3. Squeeze with fingers to form base and stand in an upright position. Alternatively, flower may be started by forming ball of paste into a pointed cone as shown in diagram 3. However, the rolled centre makes for a more attractive rose. Although this rolled centre is very simple, I find some beginners experience difficulty in mastering it, so practise stages 1 and 2 until you can do it with ease and then make the flower.

4. Finger-shape two small petals which enclose the centre. Apply the first petal, which encloses half the centre and slightly above, the second petal faces the first petal, which may be left in a closed position around the centre or for variation turned back slightly on one edge with tips of fingers. Don't forget to lightly moisten the base of each petal to attach.

5. The next stage of the rose is very important, because unless the first petal is applied correctly, the next petal will be out and so on. DO NOT apply the petal and let it flop backwards. Take a look at diagram 5 and notice how the petals stand, also the half circle shape. If you make your petals this shape, you will avoid building up below the base and creating a thick, heavy flower. This is a fault with many beginners. Apply petals this way. Attach petal in an upright position. With fingers of the left hand, hold petal on the left-hand side, and with right hand, draw the right side of petal down towards the base. That will take out the slack in the petal.

The seven stages in moulding a medium rose. The model in the lower right hand corner shows a wired flower.

34

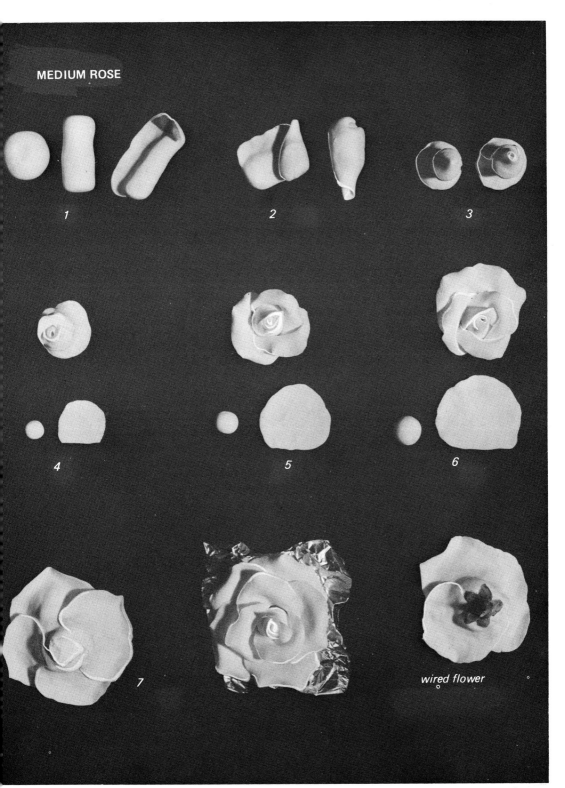

MEDIUM ROSE

1

2

3

4

5

6

7

wired flower

Now immediately curl the petal edges down on both sides with fingers, not just the top. When the flower is completed, you should be able to look into the flower and see the petals unfolding. Do not have rolled edge stand out too far, remember your next petal will be applied around it. If you curl the petals only down at the top, the flower on completion will have a cabbage formation.

Increase the size of the petals and finger-shape three petals which form the second row. Start with the first petal overlapping the second petal forming the centre. Petals are applied clockwise each petal when attached to flower overlaps the previous petal approximately half way, curling petals as each is added. If a smaller flower is required, complete at this stage.

6. Another four to six petals should complete the flower. Slightly increase the size, curling each petal into an attractive shape as you work. If you think the flower needs an extra petal, then add another and simply build on the rose until you have an attractive flower.

7. With scissors, cut away cleanly the base from the flower, leaving it nicely rounded, and place carefully in cupped alfoil to dry. **Note.** This flower may be wired. When you are able to make the flower with ease, try 'veining' the petals for a more realistic touch. I have given you in great detail the instructions for making this rose a "perfect" one, but you will find when you have mastered it each stage takes only seconds to do.

Bear in mind the following points:

(a) Aim for a good rolled centre.

(b) Thin petals to paper thickness at edge.

(c) Do not use too much moisture when applying petals.

(d) When applying petals, keep them on a level with your first two petals. If attached too high, your centre will be sunken. If attached too low, the centre will stand above the rest of the flower.

(e) Do not allow petals to come below the squeezed-in section.

Bud. If you have practised the rolled centre, then you will have no difficulty in making the bud, which is actually stage 1 and 2 of the rose. Make bud dainty, insert wire up through base, firm with fingers and cut away any surplus paste from back. When you become more proficient, you will find there will find there will be no surplus paste to cut away. Leave to dry and paint a calyx directly on to the bud. It makes a far more attractive bud than having a moulded calyx.

CECIL BRUNNER ROSE

This dainty rose teams beautifully with a number of small flowers, is ideal for a christening cake and is a great favorite of mine for wedding cakes.

The stages in moulding two types of roses: (top) Cecil Brunner rose, bud, and leaf. (bottom) English briar rose, leaf, bud and spray.

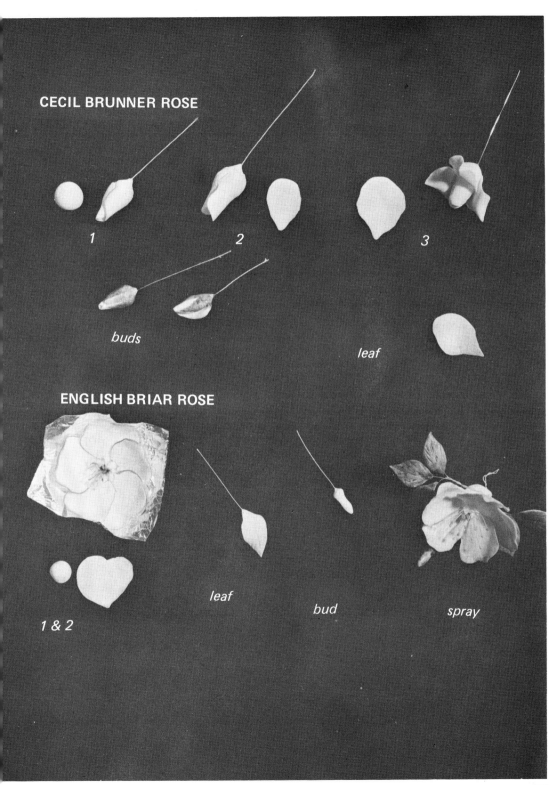

CECIL BRUNNER ROSE

1

2

3

buds

leaf

ENGLISH BRIAR ROSE

1 & 2

leaf

bud

spray

1. Roll a small centre as for medium rose, insert wire up through the base, firm with fingers and if necessary, cut away surplus paste from back.

2. Finger shape two small petals to enclose the centre. The first petal encloses half the centre and is attached so the top edge of the petal is just above the centre. The second petal faces the first petal, and for variation may be slightly turned back. Do not have the turned-back edge out too far, or you will have difficulty in applying the next three petals.

3. It takes three more petals to complete the flower, which when completed, has a distinct triangular appearance. Finger-shape, and attach each petal as it is made, pinching each petal to a point. Don't make petals too wide.

Calyx. I prefer not to add any calyx to this flower as the five-pointed calyx is quite long, and the completed flower must be handled very carefully, otherwise calyx points will be broken. If you wish to add a calyx, roll out modelling paste in pale green, cut freehand each section separately and attach. Place flower in plasticine, touch up calyx with color when dry, and leave in plasticine until required.
Bud. Mould tiny buds as stage 1, when dry paint a calyx around bud with food coloring.
Note. This rose may be painted in your choice of color. It looks lovely in shades of lemon, apricot and pink.

ENGLISH BRIAR ROSE

The English briar (Rosa canina) is a pretty shade of pink, with five almost heart-shaped petals and a mass of tiny yellow stamens.

1. Finger-shape five small petals, or roll out paste and cut out and then finger-edge. See diagram. Leave to dry.

2. Assemble and wire if desired, (see Dainty Bess rose). Mould buds and leaves small as shown in diagram. To make leaf, roll a very small piece of pale green modelling paste into a bud shape, insert wire and with fingers, flatten and point. Mark carefully over finger with scalpel, and when dry, paint. Twist three together as shown in diagram.

APPLE BLOSSOM

The apple blossom is particularly suitable for wedding and christening cakes. It is a small five-petalled flower, delicate pink, and teams with a number of tiny flowers, such as hyacinths, snowdrops, lily-of-the-valley and bluebells.
There are two methods of making this flower. Try them both and you will find one way which you prefer.

The two methods of moulding apple blossom and buttercup are shown here. In the top half is method (1) – apple blossom and buttercup, and method (2) is illustrated in the lower half.

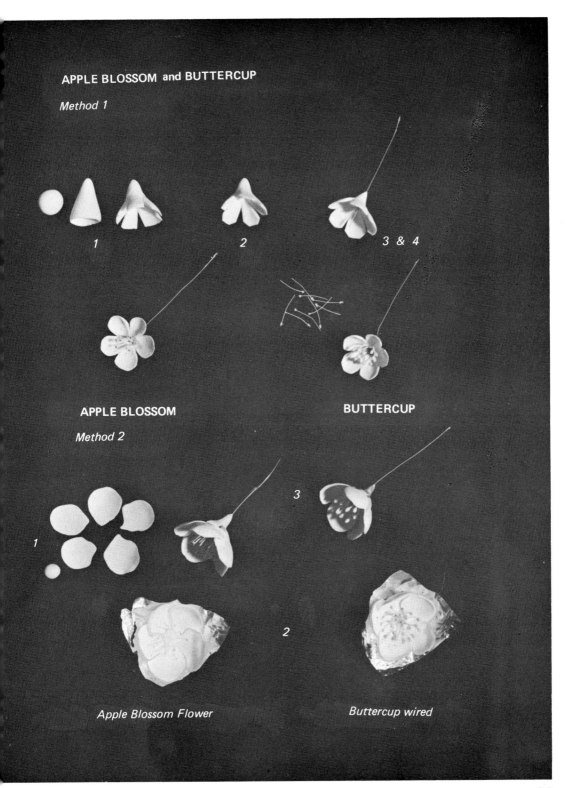

APPLE BLOSSOM and BUTTERCUP

Method 1

1

2

3 & 4

APPLE BLOSSOM

BUTTERCUP

Method 2

1

3

2

Apple Blossom Flower

Buttercup wired

Method 1. This method is easier as you can make the complete flower all at once and dispense with the use of royal icing to assemble.

1. Hollow finely a small ball of modelling paste, cut into five petals.

2. Cut off the corner of each petal, to round the top.

3. Using the rounded end of modelling stick, firmly roll and press each petal, to slightly cup it.

4. Insert wire down through the centre, firm with fingers, cut off surplus paste from back and add about eight pieces of cut stamen into the centre, bending first over fingers. When dry, paint with just a touch of pink and tip stamens red. You will not need a moulded calyx with this method, but if you wished you could paint a calyx. Flowers are wired singly into an arrangement.

Method 2.
1. Finger-shape five small petals and cup over the forefinger to give a cupped appearance. Leave to dry.

2. Assemble on alfoil. Cut a square of alfoil 4 cm (1½ inches) and pleat with fingers to give a small shallow cup in which to set the flower. Squeeze just sufficient royal icing into base and assemble petals, each petal overlapping the previous petal slightly. Add about 10 pieces of stamen stem about 1 cm (½ inch) into a small star of royal icing, and either tip red, or dip in gelatine and tip in color for a dainty appearance. See "Hints for the Decorator," page 21.

3. When flower has set, paint pale pink with a touch of soft green around the centre. Wire flower as for Dainty Bess rose, making calyx small. Flowers are inserted singly into an arrangement.

BUTTERCUP

The buttercup is a lovely fresh-looking flower and combines beautifully with red poppies, daisies, cornflowers and wheat in an arrangement of field flowers. Buttercups and daisies make an attractive spray on a birthday cake. Mould in yellow and make in the same way as apple blossom, using either method 1 or 2. Insert a lot of tiny tipped yellow stamens around the centre.
When flower has been wired, paint petals over in a lovely buttercup yellow, adding a touch of green with brown into the centre. Flowers are also wired singly into an arrangement.
Note. When making apple blossom or buttercup, method 2, make sure the petals are the correct shape, pointed and cupped, otherwise you will have difficulty in assembling.

CAMELLIA (1)

There are hundreds of varieties of camellia, so if possible, try to

Two beautiful varieties of camellia, with details of petals, leaf, and buds. Instructions for variety (2) are on page 42.

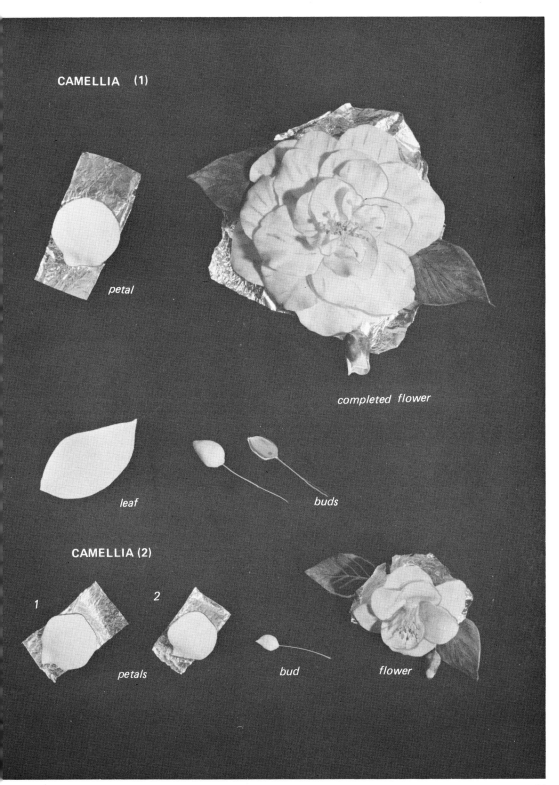

CAMELLIA (1)

petal

completed flower

leaf

buds

CAMELLIA (2)

1

2

petals

bud

flower

41

have a real flower of your choice from which to copy. One lovely camellia together with a bud and several leaves would make an attractive spray. This particular camellia has four rows of petals curved outwards with several curled petals in the centre. It is white with splashes of pink to red on the petals, and a mass of yellow stamens in the centre. The flower may be wired to take away a flat look to the arrangement. See Dainty Bess rose.

Before starting to make the flower, cut strips of alfoil on which to shape the petals. Make in the same way as for water-lily (page 102). **Note** – these strips may be put aside and used again.

1. Petals are smooth-edged. Finger-shape or cut out and finely finger the first row of five petals, and place on alfoil strips to set in a curved position. Continue same way, making each row of petals slightly smaller and shaping on curved alfoil. Make four petals for around the centre, giving a twist to each.

2. To assemble the flower. See diagram for full-blown rose. Take a square of alfoil sufficiently large enough to assemble the flower. Squeeze a circle of royal icing in the centre and position the first row of petals. Continue until all rows are positioned, each row alternating with the previous row. With tweezers, add about two dozen stamens into the centre and the four small petals. If necessary, place a piece of rolled alfoil beneath a petal to support it until the flower sets.

Bud. Mould bud to shape, insert wire and paint when dry.
Leaves are oval. Cut out finely in pale green paste, shape on alfoil and when dry, paint.

CAMELLIA (2)

This small camellia is most attractive in pastel pink with a deeper shade around the centre, and one I think a beginner will appreciate. It has two rows of four small petals.

1. Finger-shape or cut out and finger four outside petals and curve over alfoil to dry.

2. Make the second row of petals as the first row, only smaller. **To assemble flower.** Take a square of alfoil about 5 cm (2 inches) and pleat with fingers to form a shallow cone. Squeeze just enough royal icing into the centre to position the four outside petals. The second row alternates with the first row. Add a little more royal icing and with tweezers, insert about two dozen long fine-tipped stamens. Set aside to dry. This tiny camellia may be wired also.

Bud. Mould bud to shape, wire and paint when dry.
Leaves are oval and small.

GARDENIA

This lovely small white flower is an ideal one for an all-white wedding. The flower is very quickly made this way as it dispenses with the use

Step by step illustrations for moulding (top) – gardenia and leaf (centre) – bouvardia with closed flower and bud, and (bottom) – stephanotis and bud, with suggested sprays for stephanotis and bouvardia.

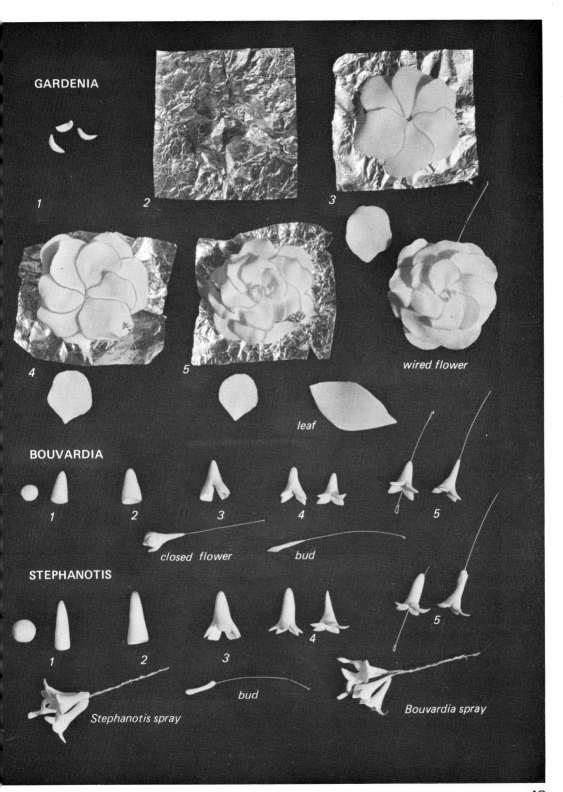

GARDENIA

1 2 3

4 5 wired flower

leaf

BOUVARDIA

1 2 3 4 5

closed flower bud

STEPHANOTIS

1 2 3 4 5

bud

Stephanotis spray Bouvardia spray

43

of royal icing in assembling. The flower has three rows of six small petals in each row and in the centre are three tiny bud-like pieces of rolled paste which may be tipped in yellow or left white.

1. Mould three pieces for the centre and allow to dry while flower is being made. Using the tiniest piece of paste, roll to form a tiny bud and bend. See diagram.

2. Take a square of alfoil about 5 cm (2 inches) and shape to form a shallow dome.

3. Finger-shape six tiny petals to form the first row, and as each petal is made, moisten the base of the back only and firmly position, each petal slightly overlapping the previous row.

4. Finger-shape the second and third row of petals, moulding the petals slightly smaller. **Note** – only a touch of moisture is required for the petal to stick. Each row of petals alternates with the previous row.

5. Lightly moisten the base of the three tiny pieces, and place into the centre.
Leave flower to completely dry, tip centre yellow, and if desired, the flower may be wired. See Dainty Bess rose.
Note – If necessary, place a piece of rolled alfoil behind a petal until set.

Leaves. Cut leaves oval, place on alfoil to set and paint.

SWEET PEA

The sweet pea is a lovely flower and I think it could be used a lot more in cake decorating than it is. Combined with spring flowers, the sweet pea makes a most attractive decoration. It may be made in all pastel colors.

1. First make the centre. Take a small piece of paste, roll between fingers to resemble a large bud, insert wire and leave to dry. Remember, the size of the completed centre will determine the size of the flower.

2. Finger-shape a petal just large enough to completely enclose the rolled centre. Moisten around all edges before applying. That makes a lovely centre.

3. Finger-shape the next petal and apply as shown in stage 3, folding the petal slightly forward.

4. Finger-shape a larger petal, thinning down the edges nice and finely, apply to flower and curl back petal edges with fingers. When dry, paint flower a pastel shade and a calyx around the base for a realistic touch.

Bud. Make stages 1 and 2.

An attractive flower not often used in cake decorating is the sweet pea, seen here in spray and bud form (top half). The stages in moulding, the violet, with bud, leaf, and spray, are on the lower half of the photograph. Instructions for violet, page 46.

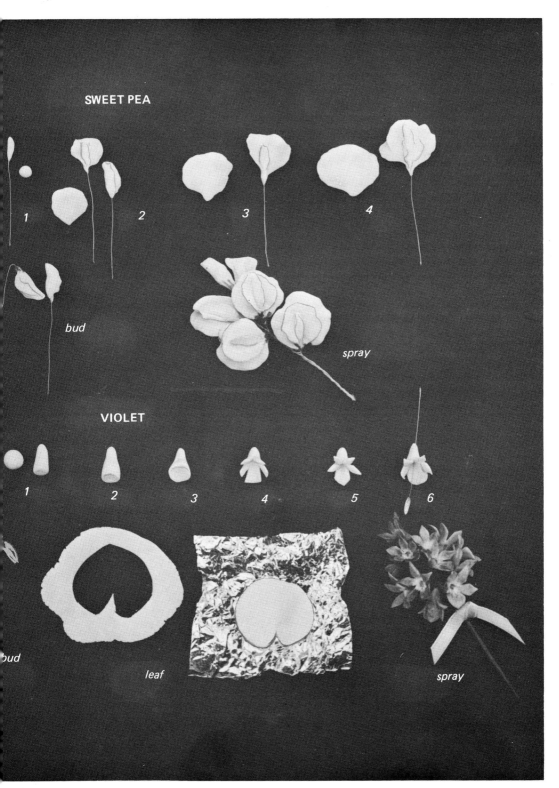

SWEET PEA

1

2

3

4

bud

spray

VIOLET

1

2

3

4

5

6

bud

leaf

spray

Partly opened flower. Make stages 1, 2 and 3.
If you are able to obtain any fine cotton-covered wire, color green and wind around a sewing needle to form tendrils. One or two may be wired in with spray when assembling.

VIOLET

Violets, sweet peas, roses and hyacinths are a lovely combination for an arrangement. The violet is so easy to make this way and dispenses with making the petals separately and assembling afterwards.

1 and 2. As for bouvardia. Mould in white and paint afterwards as there is an area of white around the centre.

3 and 4. Hollow finely with modelling stick and cut into five petals. First make two cuts well down into the flower (this represents ⅓ of the flower), and cut that section into two equal parts – that forms the two top petals. The ⅔ remaining is cut into three petals, one large centre petal and two side petals.

5. Cut each petal to a point, cutting ⅔ of the way down each side and rounding off the centre petal.

6. "Thin" each petal (this extra rolling will give you a lovely shaped petal) and insert hooked wire down through the centre of the flower, firm with fingers and taper down the wire slightly. Insert a small lemon-tipped stamen just sufficiently long enough to attach, otherwise it will come through the back of the flower. **Note** – you could use a hyacinth bud as shown in diagram 6 and tip lemon, or a dot of royal icing. Curve petals, some forward, some back as shown in flower spray. With tweezers bend flower heads forward slightly and wire singly into an arrangement.

Bud. Mould bud shape, insert wire, firm with fingers and make several cuts into the bud with scissors.
Paint flowers in shades of mauve, some pale, some in a deeper shade, leaving an area of white around the centre. Paint a touch of green at base of bud and flower.

BOUVARDIA

An attractive flower in shades of pink or white and very versatile, as it combines with any number of small and large flowers such as snowdrops, orange blossom and roses.

1. Take a pea-sized piece of modelling paste, roll between the fingers to form a cone shape about 10 mm (½ inch) and flatten top with forefinger.

2. Insert modelling stick into the centre and hollow out finely.

3. Using scissors, cut first in half and then bisect each half to form

Full blown rose – always make a few more petals than required, as some will fit together better than others. Assembly on alfoil is also shown.

46

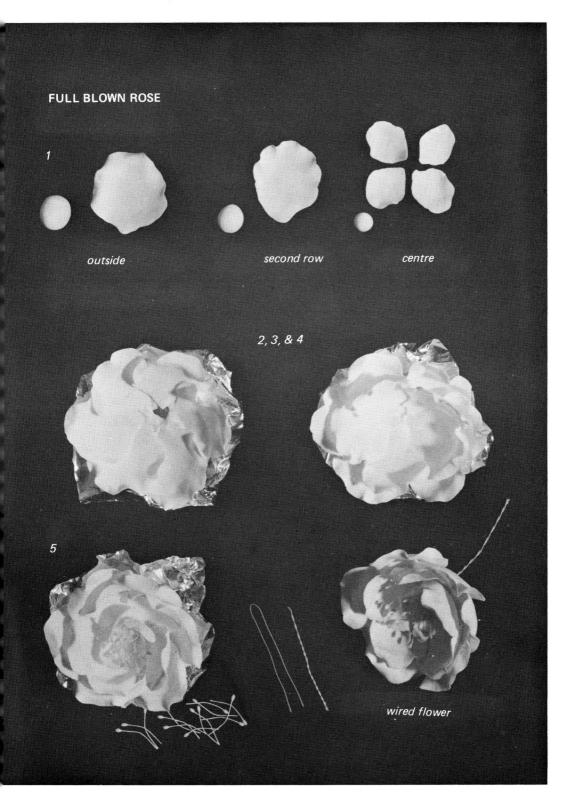

FULL BLOWN ROSE

1

outside *second row* *centre*

2, 3, & 4

5

wired flower

four petals. Place finger across the top and open out petals. That will make it easy to cut.

4. Cut each petal to a point, cutting ⅔ of the way down the sides. With thumb and forefinger, press each petal.

5. Insert wire down through the centre, firm at base with fingers and taper paste to a fine point. If necessary, cut away any surplus paste.

Closed flower. Make as for flower. Before inserting wire apply a little pressure at the base of each petal with modelling stick, insert wire and fold petals over with tips of fingers.

Bud. Using a very tiny piece of paste, mould bud shape, insert wire and taper paste to a fine point.

Twist several buds and flowers to form a small head of flowers.

STEPHANOTIS

Stephanotis is also known as Madagascar jasmine and has larger, tubular, waxy-white flowers and smooth oval leaves. If scaled down in size, it is very suitable for cake decoration. Small sprays look very dainty in a wedding arrangement.

1 to 5. Using a slightly larger ball of paste, make as for bouvardia, but this time roll between fingers to form a tubular shape about 2 cm (¾ inch) and cut five petals. If desired, a tiny calyx may be painted around base of flower.

Bud. Mould bud shape, insert wire and when dry paint a soft green, leaving tip white. If desired, buds may be left white for a wedding cake.

Twist several buds and flowers to form a small head.

FULL BLOWN ROSE

Full blown roses always make an eye-catching arrangement on a wedding, anniversary or birthday cake, whether on their own or teamed with small flowers.

No two decorators will make a rose exactly the same, so if possible, have a rose in front of you to copy while moulding the petals. In that way you will be able to see how the petals are curled and positioned.

1. A combination of six outside, five middle and four centre petals will make a lovely flower. It will, of course, depend on their shaping and how you position them when assembling. If you find you need an extra petal to give an attractive shape to the flower, then add it. Always make a few more petals than required, as some petals will fit more readily together than others. Work with a softer consistency of modelling paste to give yourself time to shape the petal and work it to paper thinness at the edge.

Finger-shape petals in three different sizes and try to obtain as much curl as possible into petal edges and so adding to the natural appearance of the completed flower.

Alternative method for making full blown rose—petals are hand moulded first, and then placed over the back of a dessert spoon or inside a teaspoon to set. Step by step directions for the Cecil Brunner rose are given below.

FULL BLOWN ROSE

1

large   medium   small

2 paint petals

3 assemble

CECIL BRUNNER ROSE — FULL BLOWN

See diagrams "veining a petal" and "shaping a petal over thumb" page 16. As each petal is completed, place in patty pan and allow to dry completely before assembling. Large petals can also be shaped over the back of a dessertspoon and small petals on the inside of a teaspoon. Try both ways.

2. To assemble. Cut a square of alfoil sufficiently large to assemble the flower, squeeze a circle of firm royal icing with a No. 5 tube and arrange the outside petals clockwise and overlapping. Now place the first two fingers of the left hand into the centre, and holding petals firmly, cup alfoil around the petals to hold in position. **Note.** Petals at this stage are positioned slightly out from the centre to avoid a build up in the centre when adding the next two rows.

3. Squeeze another ring of royal icing around the base of the first petals and position the second row.

4. Squeeze sufficient royal icing into the centre to complete the flower, and place the centre petals in position.

5. Lift rose on the alfoil and carefully rest in the hollow of patty tin. Do not push the rose into the bottom. Check with fingers to make sure all petals are firmly positioned. Using tweezers, add about two dozen finely tipped stamens (singly), curving them first over fingers to give a natural appearance. Do not add a clump of stamens all at once into the centre – that will be unattractive. Do not cut stamens too short, stamens should be about 2 cm (¾ inch).
Allow flower to completely dry before painting. Flower may also be wired. See Dainty Bess rose.

GERANIUM

This is another flower you don't see very much on decorated cakes, yet they make a beautiful decoration, easy to arrange and simple to do.

1. First make the wired calyx. Make as you would for bouvardia, mould in pale green and touch up later, but this time cut into five equal parts. After cutting down the sides, "thin" and slightly cup to take the petals as shown in diagram. Leave to set and completely dry.

2. Five small petals complete the flower. Finger-shape petals, making sure the base is pointed (diagram 2), otherwise petals will not fit into calyx. As each petal is made, position into calyx, not forgetting to lightly moisten the back of the base of the petal first. Each petal overlaps slightly the previous petal, and on completion, add several tiny pieces of cut stamen (stem only). Tip with burgundy red when dry.

Buds. Mould bud shape, insert wire up through the base, firm, and when dry, paint a tiny calyx around base of bud. Paint flowers when

Top: Simple and easy-to-arrange stages for making geraniums. Instructions for making carnation, page 52.

50

GERANIUM

1

2

3

bud

spray

CARNATION

1

2

3

4

bud

flower

51

dry, you have a choice of many pastel colors. Several buds and four or five flowers will make a nice spray. Twist wire close to flower, and with tweezers turn buds down.

Leaf. The geranium leaf adds a touch of realism to the completed spray. Roll out modelling paste in pale green, fine but not paper thin and cut out leaf shape freehand if possible. Pick up, and with fingers of both hands work right around the leaf, thinning it out nice and finely. "Vein" the leaf for a natural look, and using your scalpel lightly mark a vein in several places from the base to the rounded edge of the leaf. With the pointed end of your modelling stick work around the edge of the leaf in a rolling and pressing motion, applying more pressure in the pressing motion. This will actually give the edge a lovely fluted appearance. Also place the modelling stick (pointed end) behind the leaf in several places and pinch carefully with the fingers. This will also help to give you a fluted edge. By now the leaf should be holding its shape. Place on alfoil to dry, and when dry, paint. There are lovely markings on some geranium leaves which look most attractive.

Pelargoniums. Make as for geranium. Refer to a good garden book for colors, and be prepared to experiment with mixing colors to obtain some lovely shades.

CARNATION

The carnation is rather an exciting flower to mould and one few cake decorators will attempt. However, knowing just how to go about making it really cuts your work in half, and if you follow the detailed instructions, with practice, you too will be able to make a carnation to be proud of. Carnations make a lovely decoration on an anniversary or wedding cake.

I am going to give you two methods of making this flower, try them both. You will find one way which you prefer.

Method 1

1. First make and set the calyx on wire. Mould in pale green as you do for Christmas bell (page 92), cutting a five-pointed calyx. Hollow, insert wire, firm at base with fingers and leave to dry, then paint.

2. Finger-shape five or six petals to a nice fine edge, and as each one is made, moisten back of petal at the base, and place directly into calyx, each petal overlapping half way the previous petal. Do not make petals too large or too wide. Note the shape of the carnation petal. Try to get this shape at the base of the petal, otherwise you will fill in the calyx long before you complete the flower. If it is not quite the right shape, cut to shape with your flower scissors. Practice will correct that fault. After finger-shaping your petals, "vein" them, and don't worry if the "veining" cuts the edge here and there as it looks more natural.

3. Continue in same way, decreasing the size of petals and applying as each is made, until you have three rows of petals. Make several small petals for the centre, easing in with modelling stick. When the flower is completed, top should have a nice rounded appearance, petals with plenty of curl, and as they near the centre, be upright. If petal requires it, place a rolled piece of alfoil behind it until flower sets. For an added realistic touch, two fine "spikes" (finely rolled pieces of modelling paste) are set on wire and inserted directly into flower on completion, and just protruding slightly. Leave it out if you are unable to make it very finely.

If flower is to lie on cake, roll a stem in modelling paste to the required length, insert a short length of wire into the stem, firming with fingers. Narrow leaves may be added to hide the join. Carefully paint leaves and stem.

4. Partly opened flower. Mould in the same way, make calyx smaller, add fewer petals and make them smaller.

Bud. Mould bud to shape as shown, insert wire, leave to dry. Small calyx may be hollowed and attached, but I prefer to paint a calyx around the bud when dry.

Painting the flower. Carnations may be painted in many lovely pastel shades, but the painting must be done carefully and artistically. If possible, paint from a flower. If you prefer, you could knead a little of the main color into your modelling paste and paint the flower when completely dried. Experiment when mixing colors to obtain the correct shade. When moulding the carnation, watch for these points:

(a) Mould the correct shape of petals, particularly the outside ones. It is not so important for the centre petals. You might find it easier to make them similar in shape to the medium rose.

(b) Petals must be finely moulded or flower will look heavy.

(c) Do not apply too much moisture when adding a petal. Once the flower has set and dried, petals will be firmly positioned. Cup completed flower in alfoil and carefully pack in a box.

Method 2. This time reverse the making of the flower. Before starting, take a square of alfoil about 9 cm (3½ inches) and pleat with fingers to form a shallow cup shape, and curve back the edge. The curved edge will support the first row of petals.

Make your carnation in exactly the same way as method 1, but this time, assemble the petals as they are made in the alfoil.

Leave completed flower in alfoil until set. When thoroughly dried, remove, turn upside down and position calyx (refer method 1) and-leave to set.

HYACINTH

The hyacinth is very popular not only for wedding cakes, but it is also widely used in arrangements on special occasion cakes and may be made in many pastel colors. This is one small flower you should practise.

1 and 2. Mould as for bouvardia (page 43).

3. This time cut to form six petals, cutting well down into the throat of the flower. Cut first in half and then trisect each half.

Carnation
Method 2
First row of petals

Completed flower

Wired flower

53

4. Cut petals to a point, cutting ⅔ of the way down on either side. Groove each petal. Rest each petal in turn on the forefinger, and with modelling stick press gently but firmly along the centre of each petal in a "press and bend" movement. It will make the petals easier to curl back.

5. Insert wire down through the centre of flower, firm at base and, using the thumb and forefinger, turn back two opposite petals at one time. That means in three movements the six petals have been curled back.

This flower will require a lot of practice to perfect, and you will have to work quickly to complete it and turn back tips before icing dries. Try working with a slightly softer consistency of paste, or turning back the petals first, and then inserting the wire.

Don't worry if your flowers are a little on the big side, it is only natural with a beginner. It is far better to make a larger flower and be able to handle it, than try to make it small and ruin it before completion. When you are able to perfect the flower in a larger size, then gradually work down the ball of modelling paste used, until you are able to use a small ball.

Bud. Mould a very tiny piece of paste to shape, insert wire, firm and leave to dry.

A bud and two or three flowers may be twisted together to form a spray.

SNOWDROP

This dainty flower is well worth the effort to perfect. Tipped in green, it is an ideal small flower to add to an arrangement. It looks particularly dainty in a spray on a christening cake.

Complete up to stage 5 of the hyacinth. Now "thin" petals, cup with rounded end of modelling stick, insert wire, firm with fingers and turn petal points slightly back in some flowers and leave others cupped.

Twist a bud and several flowers to form a spray. Tiny pieces of cut stamen may be added to flower on completion and tipped yellow when dry. Finally add a touch of green to petal points and base of flower, although on the flower it is just below the tip of the petal.

LILY-OF-THE-VALLEY

This dainty flower is most suited for cake decorating and looks particularly pretty when combined with frangipani or roses, especially if sprays are arranged on a wedding cake.

It is easy to make, but takes time. I am giving you three ways to mould the tiny flower – (a) and (b) are more quickly made but look quite effective if finely moulded, (c) takes longer and is only for the more experienced decorator. I use a fine green-tipped stamen to attach each flower, but if you wish you could use a white stamen.

(a) Mould a tiny piece of modelling paste over rounded end of modelling stick. Insert stamen, firm and leave to dry.

(b) Make the same as (a) making tiny nicks around the top with

Top row: Hyacinth flower, bud, and spray. Instructions age 53.
Middle row: Snowdrop bud, flower, and spray.
Bottom row: Lilly-of-the-valley bud, flower, and spray.

54

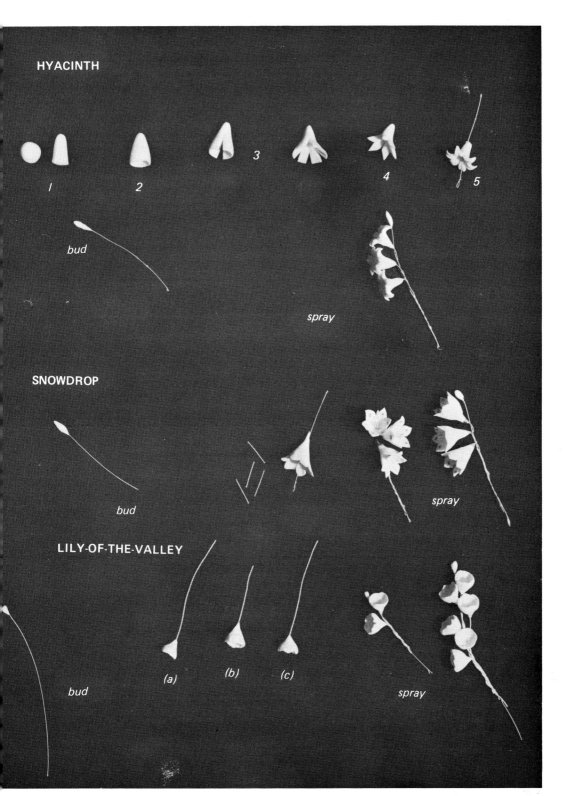

HYACINTH

1

2

3

4

5

bud

spray

SNOWDROP

bud

spray

LILY-OF-THE-VALLEY

(a)

(b)

(c)

bud

spray

scissors or pinch out with tweezers. Insert stamen.

(c) Make the same way as (a), then using rounded end of modelling stick, apply a little pressure around the inside of the edge, and carefully draw paste to form points. Do it resting on the forefinger. Reshape if necessary and insert stamen.

Bud. Use a white stamen, moisten tip and mould the tiniest piece of paste over it.

When flowers are completely set, bind as many as required on to a length of wire with either green cotton or a strip of parafilm.

ORANGE BLOSSOM

This lovely flower is very popular with brides, and teams beautifully with full-blown roses or as the main flower with either bouvardia, hyacinths or lily-of-the-valley. The flower has a fringed centre and the petals are fleshy looking. Orange blossom has from four to six petals but the accepted number is five petals.

There are two methods of making orange blossom, the first method being easier. Once again use the hollowing method, as the whole flower is then made at once, and it dispenses with the use of royal icing to assemble.

Method 1

1. Roll a ball of modelling paste between fingers and flatten top with forefinger.

2. Insert pointed end of modelling stick into the centre and hollow. Do not hollow finely at this stage. Leave a slight thickness to the petals to give you a fleshy look.

3. With scissors, cut well down into the centre to make five equal petals. Short cuts will not give you nice long petals.

4. Cut each petal to a point, cutting down the sides ⅔ of the way. Try to round the sides and avoid a sharp V effect.

5. Using thumb and forefinger as shown in diagram, firmly press each petal and bend slightly, at the same time draw the petal with the thumb towards you. This will not only shape the petal, but lengthen it, giving you beautifully moulded fine petals while still retaining the fleshy look of the orange blossom.

6a. Insert wire, firm at base and cut away any surplus. Brush a touch of yellow into the centre and using tweezers, insert three or four yellow-tipped stamens.

Method 2 – make a fringed centre. When dry, tip yellow.

1 and 2. As for bouvardia.

3. With scissors, fringe the centre as finely as possible. forming the stamens. Insert wire down through the centre and firm at base with fingers, cutting away surplus paste. Using tweezers, insert one yellow-tipped stamen just long enough to show above the centre.

Orange blossom is made in two stages. First shape centre (top row), then five-petalled flower, and assemble as shown. Bottom row shows bud, calyx, completed bud and spray.

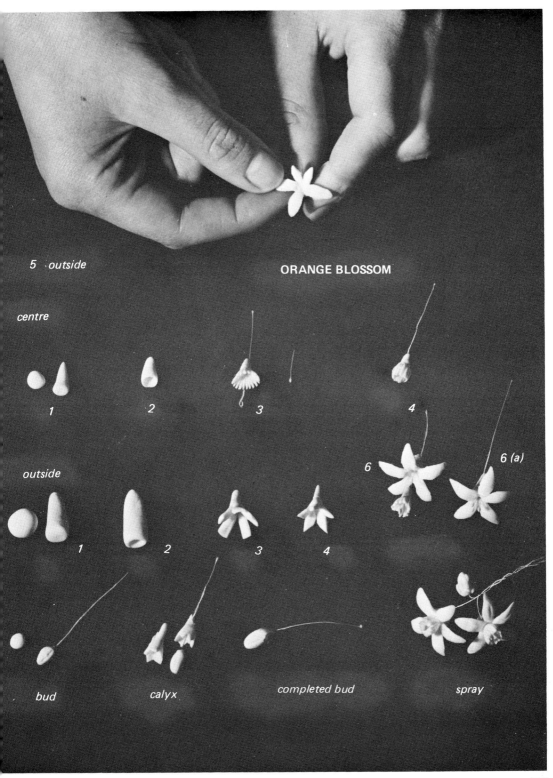

5 ·outside

ORANGE BLOSSOM

centre

1   2   3   4

6   6 (a)

outside

1   2   3   4

bud   calyx   completed bud   spray

4. When fringing, you will notice the centre fan out. After inserting wire and stamen, close centre with tips of fingers. When completely set and dried, make outside of flower as per method 1, and insert centre. See diagram 6.

Bud. Using a tiny ball of paste, shape bud, insert wire up through the base, firm and mark over the top with scissors. When dry, paint a five-pointed calyx around base. If preferred, you can mould a calyx, but keep it small. Mould in pale green as for bouvardia, cutting five points. Moisten base of bud when dry, insert down through calyx, fold points around with fingers, and cut away surplus paste from back.

Flowers may be inserted singly into cake or twisted to form a spray.

BLUEBELL

Bluebells look lovely with spring flowers, also arranged with camellias or roses.

1 to 5. Using a slightly larger ball of paste, make exactly as for hyacinth. Before inserting wire, place rounded end of modelling stick into the centre of flower and slightly cup. Insert wire, and add three yellow stamens.

Bud. Mould bud shape and wire.
Paint flowers blue, and while still wet, brush mauve through. It gives a lovely color to the flower.
Twist several buds and three or four flowers to form a spray.

ROCKERY SUCCULENT

This rockery succulent, called Echeveria gibbiflora, is moulded in yellow, has a touch of red on the outside of the petals and the calyx is a dull green with a touch of brown. It is very suitable for a masculine cake and teams well with daisies.

1. Roll a small ball of paste in yellow between fingers and flatten top.

2. Hollow finely.

3. Cut into five.

4. Cut each petal to a point.

5. Cup over rounded end of modelling stick. Insert wire down through the centre, firm with fingers, cut away surplus paste and with tweezers insert four red-tipped stamens. Leave to dry and paint outside of petals with a touch of red.

Calyx. Do not add calyx until flower has set on wire. Mould calyx in green and make as for flower. Moisten back of flower and insert into calyx. Firm with fingers and cut away surplus paste from back of flower cleanly. When dry, paint with green and brush a little brown through.
Twist one flower after another to form a spray.

Stages in moulding three small flowers. Top: Bluebell flower, bud and spray. Middle row: Rockery succulent flower, calyx, and spray. Bottom row: Primula flower, bud, and spray.

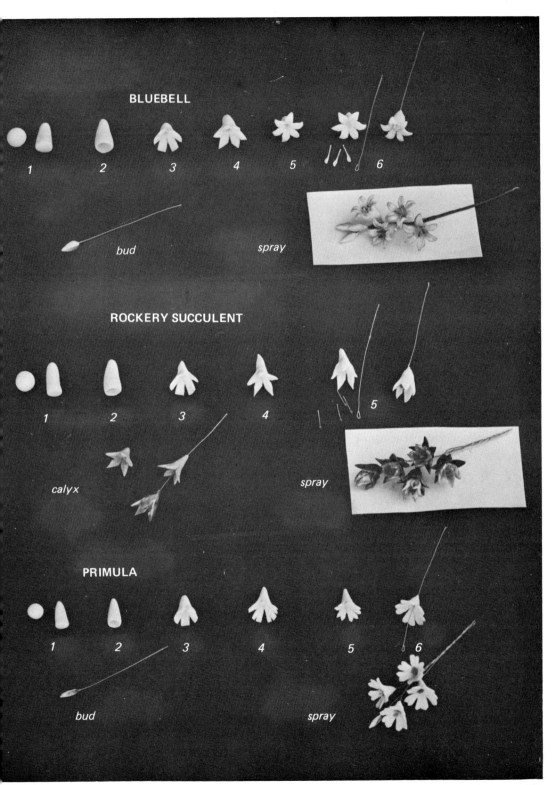

BLUEBELL

1   2   3   4   5   6

bud   *spray*

ROCKERY SUCCULENT

1   2   3   4   5

calyx   *spray*

PRIMULA

1   2   3   4   5   6

bud   *spray*

PRIMULA

Primula, a small five-petalled flower in white, pink or mauve is very suitable for arrangements on wedding or special occasion cakes.

1. Using a small ball of paste, roll between fingers and flatten top.

2. Hollow.

3. Cut into five petals, taking cuts well down.

4. Make a short cut into the centre of each petal.

5. Cut each petal to a point.

6. "Thin" each petal and insert wire. Firm at base and cut away any surplus paste. Leave to dry.

Bud. Mould shape, insert wire and when dry, paint a tiny calyx around bud.
Flowers may be left white or painted a pastel shade of pink or mauve. With brush, add a touch of yellow in the centre of the flower and a touch of green at the base.
Twist a bud and several flowers to form a spray.

FORGET-ME-NOT

This tiny flower can be moulded, and although forget-me-nots are blue, make them in any pastel shade when requiring a touch of pink, blue, apricot, mauve or other to match bridesmaids' frocks. They look delightful in an arrangement on a christening cake. The flower is very simple to make, but attempt it only when you are able to handle a very tiny piece of paste.

1. Using a very tiny ball of paste, roll between fingers to form a tiny cone shape and flatten top with finger to resemble a tack.

2. With scissors make five tiny cuts around the edge into the centre. As this flower is so tiny, I have made stage 2 on a larger scale and marked the cuts with color.

3. With thumb and forefinger, draw out each section to form a tiny petal.

4. Insert wire, firm at base and insert head of lemon stamen with just sufficient stem to attach. Hold scissors firmly behind flower and take away surplus paste. Wire flowers singly into an arrangement, just scattering through the spray. **Note** – Stamens may be any color to match color of flower.

JASMINE

This beautiful flower looks lovely on a wedding cake because of its

A selection of dainty flowers to mould: Top: Forget-me-not flower and spray. Middle row: Jasmine flower, spray, and buds. Bottom row: Lilac flower, two sizes of buds and completed spray.

60

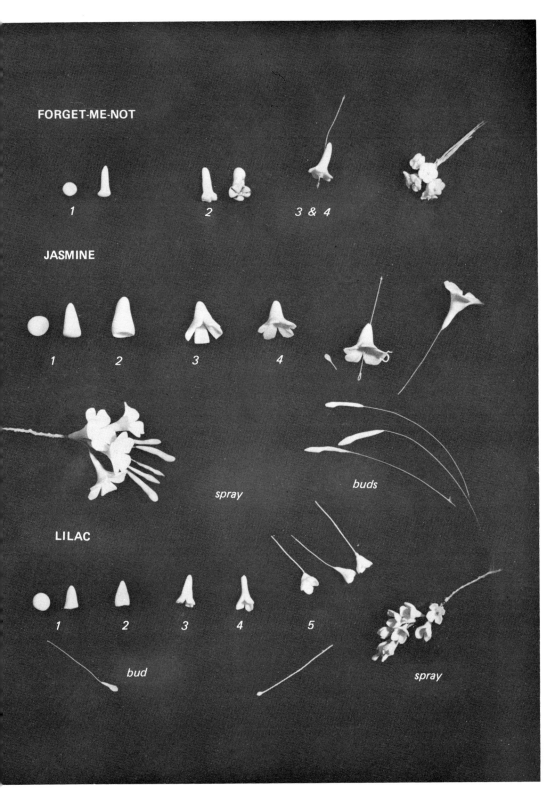

FORGET-ME-NOT

1

2

3 & 4

JASMINE

1   *2*   *3*   *4*

spray

buds

LILAC

1   *2*   *3*   *4*   *5*

bud

spray

dainty appearance and soft coloring. It blends particularly with full-blown roses.

1 and 2. Mould as for bouvardia.

3. Insert modelling stick and this time hollow and cut into five equal petals, cutting well down into the flower.

4. With scissors, cut off each corner of each petal to give a rounded top.

5. "Thin" and insert wire down through the centre of the flower, firm with fingers and taper paste down the wire to a nice fine point. Immediately add one fine-tipped white stamen, which comes just above centre of flower.

Bud. Mould buds various sizes. Using a tiny ball of paste, roll between fingers just below the top, that will shape the bud, then taper down to a point. Paint buds when dry a deep shade of pink, base soft green with just a touch of brown brushed through. Paint flowers just a touch of pale pink underneath petals and down to the base of flower, add a touch of green around the base.
Twist four or five buds and two to four flowers for a spray.

LILAC

Small sprays of lilac can be used when wishing to add a touch of mauve to an arrangement. Attempt this flower only when you are able to handle a very tiny piece of modelling paste, as the flowers are so small.

1 to 4. Make as for bouvardia, and when shaping petals with scissors, just cut off the corners of each petal to give a rounded top. This time, cup each tiny petal by firmly pressing with rounded end of modelling stick.

5. Insert either wire or small yellow-tipped stamen and leave to dry, cutting away surplus paste from back.

Bud. Mould pieces of paste to form a bud, and wire. If flowers are set on wire, twist several flowers to form a spray. When dry, paint in shades of mauve and a touch of yellow in the centre. If flowers are set on a stamen, bind to a length of fine wire with green cotton.

FUCHSIA

Fuchsias make lovely arrangements on cakes for any special occasion, and may be made in shades of mauves and pinks, also white. They look superb on a wedding cake, particularly the double fuchsia. This flower is one which should be constantly practised.
There are two methods of making this flower – try both.

Single fuchsia – Method 1

1. Take eight long, small-tipped stamens and one longer stamen

Single fuchsia, method 1 (top), and method 2 (below).

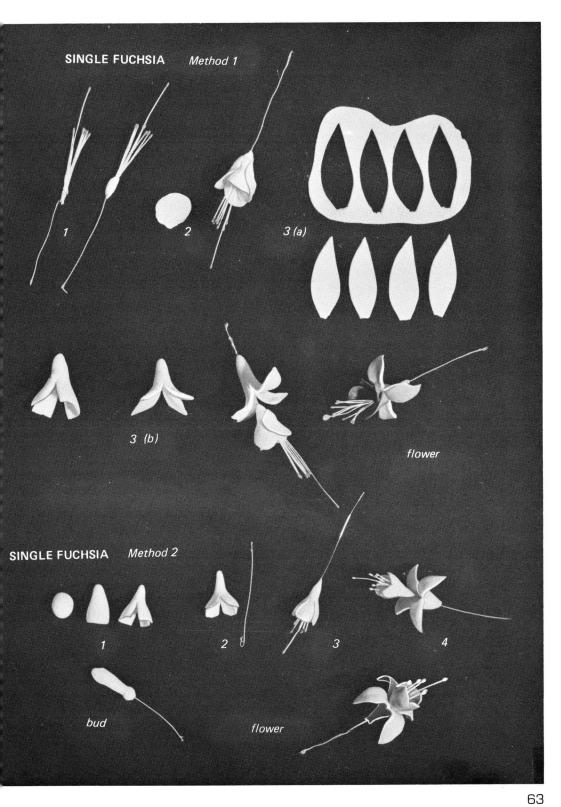

SINGLE FUCHSIA *Method 1*

1

2

3 (a)

3 (b)

flower

SINGLE FUCHSIA *Method 2*

1

2

3

4

bud

flower

63

and bind around the base with a length of wire to secure and make the stem. Don't cut stamens too short – they should come well out of the flower.

2. Finger-shape four small petals and attach clockwise around the centre as each one is made, each petal slightly overlapping the previous one. Allow to completely set before adding the outside petals.

3. The outside petals may be made by one of two methods.
(a) Roll out modelling paste finely, freehand-cut four petals and attach at base of flower. Mould with fingers and taper down the wire.
(b) Roll small ball of paste into a long cone, hollow, cut into four, cutting well down, and cut each petal to a point. Press with thumb and forefinger to complete shaping, moisten back of centre and insert into base. Firm with fingers and taper paste down the wire. A very tiny piece of paste is moulded around the base of flower and painted soft green. Alternatively, simply brush a touch of green around the base.

Single fuchsia – Method 2
1. Using a small ball of paste for the centre, hollow finely and cut into four.

2. With scissors, cut off each corner of each petal to give a rounded top, and roll the rounded end of modelling stick across each petal to shape.

3. Insert wire down through the centre, firm around base with fingers and with tweezers, add the stamens. Close petals around the centre and cut away any surplus paste. Leave to dry.

4. Outside petals – same as for No. 3 method 1.

Bud. Mould bud to shape, wire and when dry, paint.

DOUBLE FUCHSIA

Method 1
1. Take your stamens and wire them as for single fuchsia.

2. Finger-shape eight small petals, gradually increasing the size, and attach as each one is made. Petals overlap slightly the previous petals. Finally add four tiny petals around the base, turning slightly downwards to complete the centre.

3. Make outside petals as single fuchsia, method 1 (3).

Method 2
1. Mould the outside petals first – single fuchsia, method 1, stage 3b. Before inserting wire, place rounded end of modelling stick into the centre to slightly cup it to allow for the petals. Leave to completely dry.

Double fuchsia, method (1) top row, and method (2) middle row. Tiny ballerina fuchsia, instructions page 66.

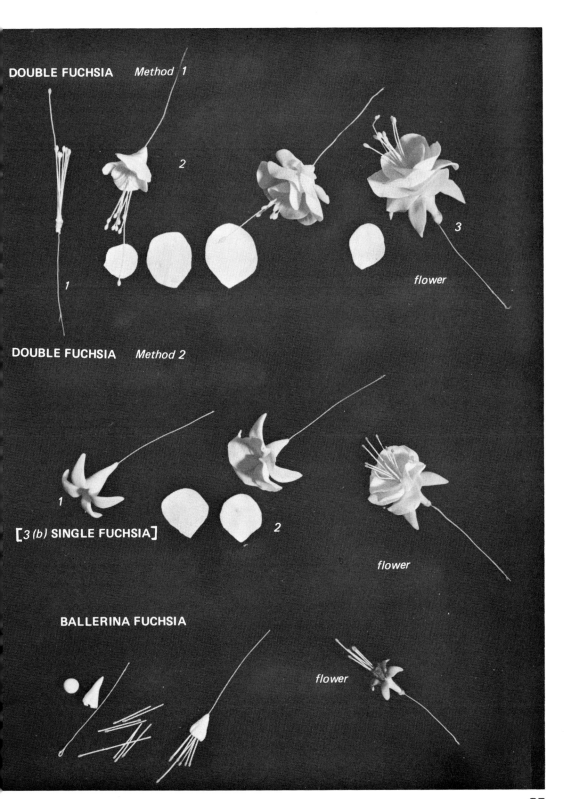

DOUBLE FUCHSIA *Method 1*

2

3

flower

1

DOUBLE FUCHSIA *Method 2*

1

[3 *(b)* **SINGLE FUCHSIA**]

2

flower

BALLERINA FUCHSIA

flower

2. Finger-shape about eight small petals and position clockwise as each one is made. Make petals smaller towards the centre. Add stamens directly into the centre of the flower upon completion.
Note. The double fuchsia must be finely moulded, otherwise the flower will look heavy.
Flowers are inserted singly into an arrangement.

BALLERINA FUCHSIA

This tiny fuchsia has a purple centre and pink outside petals and is very dainty for a christening cake, and lovely for a fill-in flower in a mixed arrangement.
This is a miniature form of the single fuchsia, make as method 1.
Note. The centre of this fuchsia is so tiny there is no need to round the petals. After cutting into four, insert wire and stamens.

JONQUIL

Jonquils combined with daisies are very suitable for a masculine cake. They look lovely with spring flowers, such as daffodils, violets, hyacinths and primulas. Flowers are white, cream, yellow centre with cream outside petals or orange centre with yellow outside petals.

1. Take a small ball of modelling paste and finely shape over rounded end of modelling stick to form the centre. Leave a little thickness at the base to secure the wire. Insert wire down through the centre and with tweezers, add three orange-tipped stamens. Cut away surplus paste and leave to dry.

2. Six small pointed petals form the outside of the flower and are arranged in two sets of three. Using a small ball of paste, roll between fingers to form a cone and flatten top with finger. Insert modelling stick (pointed end), hollow, and using tweezers, cut down to make three petals. Cut each petal to a point, rounding the sides, and with fingers pinch each petal to shape (diagram 2). Insert centre, not forgetting to moisten the base so it will stick. Firm with fingers and cut away cleanly surplus paste from back, otherwise you will not be able to position the second set of petals.

3. Make a second set of petals in the same manner, lightly moisten base of first set and insert into second set, alternating the petals and tapering paste down the wire. You might find it necessary when attaching the three petals to cut at base and ease the paste around with your fingers. When dry, mould the tiniest piece of paste around the base of the flower.
An alternative method of applying outside petals to flower is to either finger-shape or cut out each petal and attach to centre of flower separately.

Partly opened flower. Hollow small ball of modelling paste, cut into six small petals, "thin" petals, insert wire, add three stamens and close petals over with tips of fingers. Taper paste down the wire

Top: Jonquil with partly opened flower and bud, and suggested spray. Bottom: Daffodil in various stages of assembly.

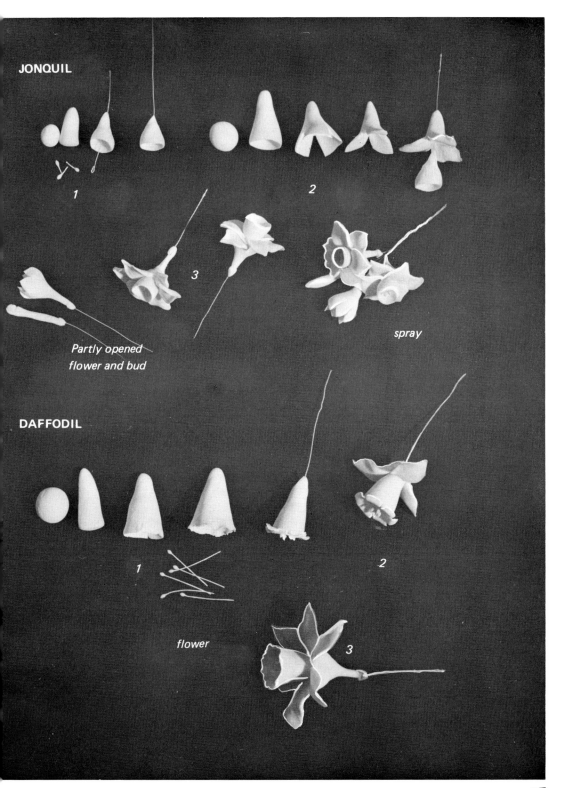

JONQUIL

1

2

3

Partly opened
flower and bud

spray

DAFFODIL

1

2

flower

3

67

and when dry add tiny piece of paste around the base.

Bud. Roll a tiny piece of paste to form bud, insert wire and make several cuts over the top with scissors. Finish base in the same way as flowers.

When dry, paint flowers adding a touch of green around base. Flowers may be inserted singly into an arrangement or several twisted together to form a spray.

DAFFODIL

The daffodil is a lovely flower and something different if yellow is the main color in your arrangement. A beautiful arrangement of spring flowers can be made using daffodils as shown in chapter 5 "Flower Sprays and Arrangements" No. 4. This type of arrangement gives you the opportunity to use up all those odd flowers you may have stored away.

The daffodil is made in a similar manner to the jonquil, except you will be handling a larger ball of modelling paste as the trumpet of flower is longer and larger, and outside petals are quite long.

1. Use a larger ball of modelling paste, roll between fingers to form a cone and flatten with top of finger. Pierce centre with modelling stick, then hollow bell shape with the rounded end. Using scissors, make six small nicks around the edge of the trumpet, or flute the edge by applying extra pressure with the modelling stick, and roll back the edge with fingers. All daffodils do not roll back, so fluted trumpet may be left upright. Insert wire down through the centre, and with tweezers, add six yellow-tipped stamens into the base of the flower, which do not extend beyond the top of the trumpet. Adding the stamens now dispenses with the use of royal icing to complete the flower later. Leave to completely set on wire before adding outside petals, otherwise when adding the centre will be formed off the wire. Cut away cleanly any surplus paste from base.

2. Using a larger ball of paste, make petals in the same manner as for jonquil. Roll to a longer cone, and when cutting petals to a point, try to curve the sides and avoid a straight cut to give a nicer shaped petal. "Thin" and "vein" the petals for a realistic appearance. Moisten base of centre and insert into petals. Firm with fingers and cut away surplus paste cleanly, otherwise the second set of petals will not "sit" well behind. Curl petals with fingers to give a natural appearance. If you are a beginner, leave to completely set. You will find it a lot easier when attaching the second set of petals.

3. Make a second set of petals in the same manner, which alternate with the first set. When attaching, cut down one side and ease it around with your fingers. Taper paste down the wire, cutting away any surplus, and if necessary, stand flower upside down while outside petals set. Mould tiny piece of paste around base and tip green. Alternatively, roll out modelling paste finely and freehand cut petals, applying each one separately. Try both methods to see which way suits you better.

Three flowers for the experienced decorator. Top: Viburnum partly opened flower, bud, and spray. Middle row: Geralton wax buds, leaf, flower, and assembled spray. Bottom: Escallonia bud, assembly of flower, calyx, and spray. Instructions, page 70-71.

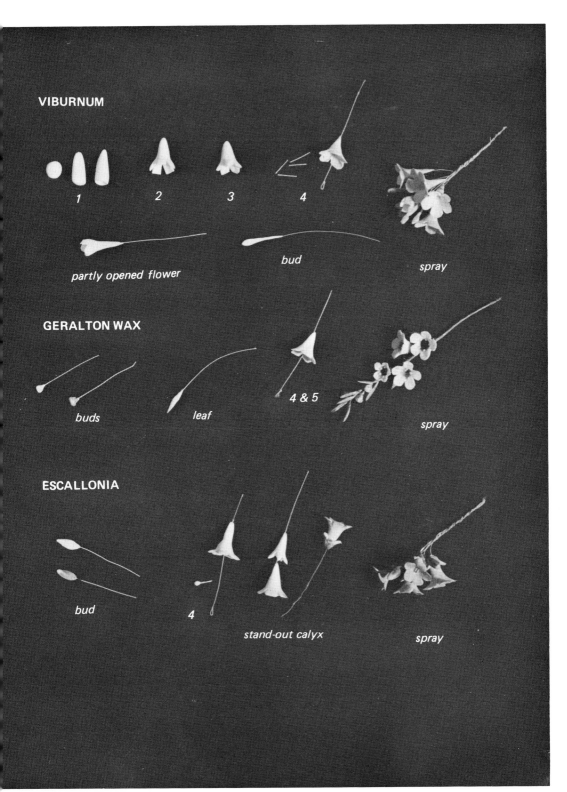

VIBURNUM

1   2   3   4

partly opened flower   bud   spray

GERALTON WAX

buds   leaf   4 & 5   spray

ESCALLONIA

bud   4   stand-out calyx   spray

Flowers are wired singly into an arrangement. I prefer to mould the flower in white and paint afterwards.

VIBURNUM

There are several varieties of Viburnum, this particular variety (Viburnum tinus) forms a head of pink and white flowers. You will find this a very versatile flower combining well with any number of flowers, but only the more experienced decorator should attempt it.

1. Using a small ball of modelling paste, roll between fingers to form a cone, and hollow it.

2. Cut to form five tiny petals.

3. Cut off corners from each petal to give a rounded top and press with thumb and forefinger.

4. Insert wire and taper down to a nice fine point. With tweezers, insert four small pieces of cut stamen stem, tip yellow when dry.

Partly opened flower. The spray looks more interesting with several partly opened flowers and buds. Using a very tiny piece of paste, make as for flower. Insert wire, firm with fingers and close over petals.

Bud. Mould bud to shape, insert wire and leave to dry.

Paint back of flowers only in a soft apricot-pink, leaving tops of petals white. Add a touch of green around base of flowers and buds. Twist several flowers and buds together to form a small head of flowers.

GERALTON WAX

This colorful tiny flower is an attractive addition to a birthday or wedding cake spray. Do not attempt this flower until you are proficient in making small flowers.

1 to 3. As viburnum.

4. Place the rounded end of modelling stick into the centre to form a small shallow cup.

5. Insert wire down through the centre, firm with fingers and cut away surplus paste from back. Leave to dry.

Petals are palest pink, centre burgundy. Pipe a tiny dot of royal icing at the base of each petal and one in the centre and tip yellow.

Buds are small and round, tipped pink and a touch of green around base.

Several buds and flowers twisted together or bound with green cotton will make a nice spray. A tiny spiked leaf may be added to spray if desired. Roll a tiny piece of paste between fingers, insert wire, flatten and point. Paint when dry.

ESCALLONIA

This dainty flower, deep pink, is very suitable to add to a spray on a special occasion cake, and should be attempted only by the more experienced decorator.

1 to 3. As viburnum.

4. Insert wire and taper flower slightly down the wire to form a small bell. With tweezers, insert one green-tipped stamen in the centre and cut away surplus paste.

To make the stand-out calyx
Using a very tiny piece of paste, make as for flower, cutting to a point. Moisten slightly base of flower and insert into calyx. Firm with fingers, open out calyx points and cut away surplus paste cleanly from back.
When dry, paint flower and top of calyx a deep pink and back of calyx green. Twist several buds and flowers to form a spray.

DAISY

A really delightful flower, looks wonderful on wedding cakes and very popular with spring brides. This is one flower which should go on your "list to perfect". It can be made in many pastel colors, pinks, mauve, cream, yellow or blues, which make it so versatile for flower arrangements. I prefer to paint after flowers are made, but of course, it is up to the individual and you may prefer to mould in color.

1. First make the centre. It is a good idea to make several dozen – they will keep indefinitely and are on hand when required. There are two ways of making a centre. (a) Use firm modelling paste, mould in yellow, (pale, touch up later if required) and roll into a small ball – about the size of a pea. Place inside a piece of tulle and twist the tulle firmly fron behind, forcing the icing slightly through the holes. Remove, insert wire, firm with fingers and leave to dry. **Note,** if modelling paste is not firm, it will stick to the tulle. Try lightly dabbing centre first in cornflour. (b) Shape modelling paste into a small ball, insert wire, firm with fingers and leave to dry. When dry, dip top first in egg white, tap lightly on a towel to remove surplus egg white and then dip in sieved lemon jelly crystals. Place on waxed paper to dry. It makes a lovely centre for the daisy.
Remember the size of the centre will determine the size of the flower, so don't make centres too large. Have you remembered to moisten the wire before attaching the centre? If not, when completing the flower in the next stages, the centre will drop off the wire.

2. Take a marble-sized piece of paste and mould stages 1 and 2 of bouvardia, but do not hollow finely at this stage.

3. Using scissors, cut first in half, taking cuts well down into the centre, but leave enough to hold the flower. That applies to any flower when hollowing. Now cut each half into five to give you ten petals.

4. Notice in stage 3 petals still have a little thickness. That will enable you to cut your petals and shape them without breaking off at the base. Using scissors, cut each petal to a point, cutting ⅔ of the way down. If you want a more rounded top, just snip off each corner.

5. "Thin" petals, taking point of modelling stick down into the centre of the flower so you won't break off any petals.

6. Moisten back of centre and insert down through the petals, and with fingers firm petals around the centre. Cut away surplus paste from the back and refirm with fingers. Leave to dry.

For a partly opened daisy, make a small centre, and on completion of flower, simply close petals around the centre with tips of fingers. Flowers are wired singly into an arrangement. Pack away carefully to avoid breaking petal points.

Michaelmas daisy. This tiny daisy is ideal to use as a small flower in an arrangement and is lovely on a christening cake.
Make a very tiny centre. Outside is made exactly the same way as an orange blossom centre. After fringing insert tiny centre and firm with fingers. Handle carefully.

FLANNEL FLOWER

The flannel flower is very suited to cake decoration and makes an eye-catching spray when used in an arrangement of Australian wildflowers. I have even had a request for a spray of flannel flowers on a wedding cake.
Make exactly as for daisy, but this time cut petals longer and, when cutting down, cut so you will have some petals shorter and some narrower. After applying petals, curve and twist some for a realistic appearance. If necessary, stand on the head to set.

Painting. First brush top of petals over with a little water to which has been added a drop of yellow food coloring. It is only faint, to give an off-white appearance to the petals and is barely noticeable. Now, while still wet, brush a little soft green towards the tips and touch the centre in soft green and a touch of brown.
Flowers are wired singly into an arrangement.

WHEAT

Should you wish to make an arrangement of field flowers, then wheat makes a very attractive addition to the spray. It is quickly moulded and simple to make, but you will need to make about three dozen for each sheaf, depending on the length required.

Various stages of assembly for daisy, Michaelmas daisy, flannel flower, and wheat.

1. Mould a very tiny piece of yellow modelling paste into a ball and thread on to a piece of stamen as shown in diagram. Roll lightly

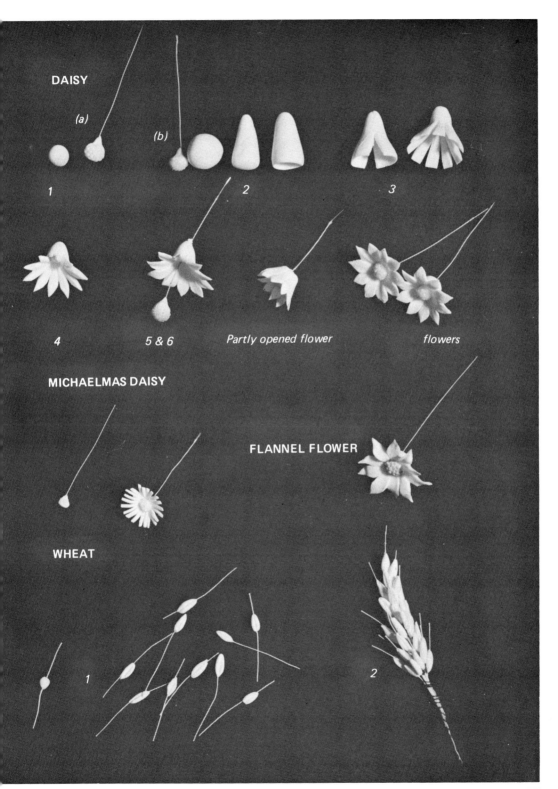

DAISY

(a)

(b)

1

2

3

4

5 & 6

Partly opened flower

flowers

MICHAELMAS DAISY

FLANNEL FLOWER

WHEAT

1

2

between fingers and resting on forefinger, mark down the centre with a scalpel. There is no need to have the stamen piece coming from every one, just enough for an effect. Have modelling paste so it will adhere to the stamen. Keep fingers lightly dusted with cornflour. Leave to dry.

2. Bind in a spiral effect to a length of wire with green cotton. Touch up in color if necessary.

PANSY

This is another flower which can be made without the use of royal icing to assemble. There are many attractive color combinations which can be used, and I suggest you refer to a good flower book. The viola is made in exactly the same way, only smaller. The flower has five petals – two back petals, two side petals and a large fluted petal.

1. First make the calyx, set on wire and completely dry. Using a small ball of pale green modelling paste, hollow and cut into five. Cut each section to a point, insert wire, firm and dry in a cupped position.

2. Finger-shape or cut out the two back petals. As each petal is made, finger edge finely, "flute", and position into calyx, first moistening the back of the base of petal only. The right petal is positioned first, then the left, which slightly overlaps the right. Cut a square of alfoil about 6 cm (2½ inches), place wire stem through and stand in a small medicine bottle. Cup the alfoil in position to support petals until flower sets.

3. Next make the two side petals in the same way, firming into position with modelling stick.

4. Finally finger-shape the centre petal and position. Place point of modelling stick into the centre, and with a little pressure, groove the centre petal at the base.
Allow to completely dry, then paint in your own choice of color.

POPPY

You will find this flower very simple to make if you have already made flowers such as Dainty Bess rose and full-blown rose. The red poppy makes a very colorful addition to a field flower arrangement. It has four petals, but it would not matter if you made five, so long as you achieve a nice shape to the flower.

1. Finger-shape or cut out petals and finely finger, "vein" and flute, and place in patty pan to set.
When petals are thoroughly dry, carefully paint red with a shading of yellow-green at the base. When dry, assemble on a square of alfoil the same as Dainty Bess rose. With tweezers, insert about three dozen fine black-tipped stamens.

A bright and colorful trio: Pansy, poppy, and cornflower.

PANSY

1

2

3

flower

4

POPPY

CORNFLOWER

1

2

3

flower

CORNFLOWER

Cornflowers are a deep blue and make a lovely addition to a field flower arrangement of poppies, wheat, daisies and buttercups. Make the flower in pale blue, and when dry, paint. Beginners might find it easier to first set a small bud on the wire. It will give you a base on which to attach the petals. Work quickly, otherwise the paste will dry before the flower is completed. You will find it easier to add the stamens as the flower is made, and trim around the base of the flower with scissors as you work. Don't get a build-up around the base of flower.

1. Roll out a tiny piece of paste just sufficient to cut one petal at a time – 2.5 cm (1 inch) long and 1 cm (⅜ inch) deep. **Note.** Although the exercise shows a piece of paste cut out accurately, it is not at all necessary to do so. So long as the piece of paste is finely moulded, particularly along the top edge, kept short and shallow in depth, is all that is required. The piece of paste can be picked up and trimmed with scissors when fringing. Use either pinking shears or scissors to cut top edge.

2. Pleat quickly with fingers and attach to wire. Don't forget to moisten. You will require about eight petals and the same number of fine black-tipped stamens to complete the flower. With scissors, trim back for a dainty appearance.

3. When dry, paint flower. Add a touch of mauve to blue for correct color.

DAPHNE

The flowers are four-sepalled and vary in color from pale lilac-pink to a deeper shade, the color being on the back of the flower. This is a flower well worth the effort to make, but attempt it only when you are proficient in making small flowers.

1. Using a pea-sized piece of paste, hollow, cut into two equal parts and open out with thumb.

2. Cut each petal to a point, cutting ⅔ of the way down and slightly curving the sides.

3. "Thin". Insert wire and pinch petals to a point. With tweezers insert four pieces of stamen. Make sure **all** surplus paste is cleanly cut away from the base, otherwise the next pair of petals will not sit properly. Leave to completely dry before adding the next set.

4. Make another set of petals in exactly the same way. Moisten the base of the first set and insert into the second set. If necessary, slit down the side and ease around base with fingers. Firm, and cut away any surplus paste from back.

Partly opened flower. Using a smaller ball of paste than that used for the flower, hollow and cut into four. Shape petals the same way, insert wire and firm with fingers. Pinch petals to a point, and lightly squeeze the two opposite petals to give the correct shape to the flower. Cut away surplus paste.

Bud. Mould bud shape and insert wire. For bud just opening, hollow very tiny piece of paste, make four small cuts, shape, insert wire and fold points around the centre.
Leaves are long, oval and pointed.
When flowers are dry, paint buds a deep shade of lilac-pink and flowers in a softer shade on the backs only. Tip stamens yellow. A mixture of mauve and a touch of red will give you the correct color. Assemble several buds, partly opened flowers and flowers to form a small head of flowers, and either twist or bind with green cotton.

GOLDFUSSIA

This pretty bell-shaped tiny flower is a lovely pale mauve. It is very dainty in an arrangement if a touch of mauve is required.

1 to 3. As for bouvardia.

4. Cut off the corners of each petal to give a rounded top. Press each section with thumb and forefinger.

5. Reshape centre if necessary to form a small bell. Insert wire, firm, cut away any surplus paste and with tweezers add four pieces of cut stamen stem. Leave to dry.

Bud. Mould bud shape as shown, insert wire. Tip bud a deeper mauve than flowers and add a touch of green around base. Paint flowers a delicate mauve and tip stamens yellow.
Note. A wired leaf may be added if desired. Mould leaf and immediately press on to wire which has been dipped in egg white and leave to dry. Handle carefully.
Twist several flowers and buds to form a spray as shown.

HONEYSUCKLE

This is a very dainty flower which will combine with many flowers to form an attractive spray. Attempt this flower only when you have perfected a number of small flowers.

1. Using a small ball of paste, roll between fingers to form a thin tubular shape about 2.5 cm (1 inch).

2. Hollow out.

3. Make two long cuts to form a petal, and three short cuts into the remainder to form four small petals.

4. Cut each petal to a point.

5. Using modelling stick "thin" petals.

6. Insert wire down through the centre, firm with fingers, and with tweezers, add six long pieces of stamen stem (one slightly longer), curving over finger first. Leave to dry.

Buds. Mould buds to shape – see diagram.
Paint backs of flowers with a touch of pink, tip stamens yellow, long stamen green and base of flower. Paint small buds pale green, larger buds, same as flowers.
Twist buds and flowers to form a spray.

KURRAJONG

This colorful wildflower looks very attractive in a wildflower arrangement and is simple to make.

1. Using a small ball of modelling paste, mould in white and hollow.

2. Cut into five short petals.

3. Cut each petal to a point.

4. With thumb and forefinger, press each petal out. Using modelling stick, hollow slightly and insert wire. Hold flower a little down from the base and swivel between fingers to form a rounded back to the flower, and taper paste to a fine point. Using tweezers, add five stamen pieces.

5. Leave to dry. Paint outside of flower with burgundy red, leaving top white. Tip stamens red.

Bud. Mould bud shape. When dry, paint a five-petalled calyx in burgundy red.

APPLE BERRY

The apple berry is yellow and white and made in a similar manner to the kurrajong.

1 to 3. As for kurrajong, but when shaping petals, cut off the corners of each petal to give a rounded top.

4 and 5. As for kurrajong, but insert three green-tipped stamens to come just above the centre.
When dry, paint flower yellow underneath, leaving top white.

Bud. Mould a round bud, insert wire and paint yellow when dry, with just a touch of green around base.

MOUNTAIN DEVIL

This easy-to-make wildflower should be added to your list of wildflowers. Seven pieces of modelling paste are rolled and joined to form the flower, with long black stamen in the centre.

1. Roll a very tiny piece of modelling on the palm of your hand into a

Daphne, Goldfussia, and Honeysuckle instructions on pages 76 and 77.

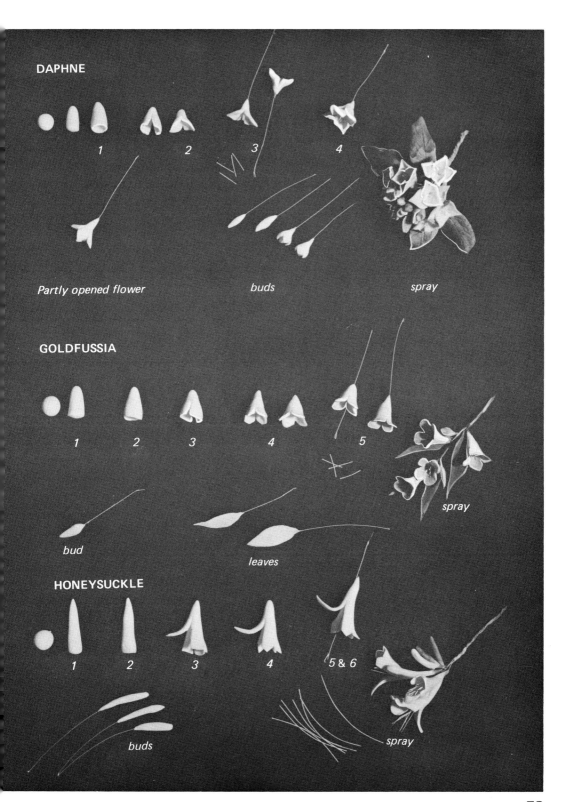

DAPHNE

1   2   3   4

Partly opened flower   *buds*   *spray*

GOLDFUSSIA

1   2   3   4   5

spray

bud   *leaves*

HONEYSUCKLE

1   2   3   4   5 & 6

buds   *spray*

79

fine strip about 2.5 cm (1 inch). Make seven and combine to form the flower with just a touch of moisture.

2. Insert wire up through the base, firm with fingers and insert one long black stamen in the centre. Leave to dry. Paint flower in burgundy pink, leaving top white and add a dot of royal icing on the top of each rolled strip.

WARATAH

The waratah is a bright spot in a wildflower arrangement. Like the orchid, this flower can look very "hard" unless moulded well and the outside petals arranged as naturally as possible. I make this flower on a toothpick (a sharpened match will do). This method dispenses with the use of royal icing to assemble the flower, makes it easier to attach the petals, paint the flower, and it elevates the flower in an arrangement.

You will find it easier to mould in color. Red powder is better, or use liquid color and make centre in deep pink and touch up afterwards.

1. First make the centre. Using a large marble-sized piece of paste, mould to a dome shape and insert toothpick and firm. Don't forget to moisten first. Pierce underneath in several places to allow the air to dry centre, and leave to completely dry.

2. Using a No. 0 or No. 1 tube, pipe dots over dome, starting at the top. Increase size as you work down with a squeeze and pull motion, just like a comma. Leave to dry.

3. Make three rows of petals with seven to nine petals in each row, each row alternating with the previous row. The number of petals will depend on the size of the dome. Finger-shape or cut out petals, and attach with a little moisture to centre as each petal is made. If you are a beginner, I would advise letting each row dry before adding the next.

4. Make the second row slightly larger and attach, alternating with the first row, and start to curl one or two petals.

5. Finally add third row slightly larger and curl outwards to give a natural appearance to the flower.

Painting. When dry, retouch with brush. Paint dome red with a touch of green and brown towards the top. Also a touch of brown through some of the petals.

Leaves are long and serrated.

NATIVE FUCHSIA

The Native Fuchsia or Fuchsia Heath is a native plant from New South Wales. It is a dainty tubular red flower tipped with white. It is very easy to make, and one to add to your wildflower list.

1. Using a very small ball of paste, roll between fingers to make a long thin tubular shape about 2.5 cm (1 inch).

Designs for a wildflower arrangement. Instructions for Kurrajong flower, apple berry, and mountain devil are on page 78.

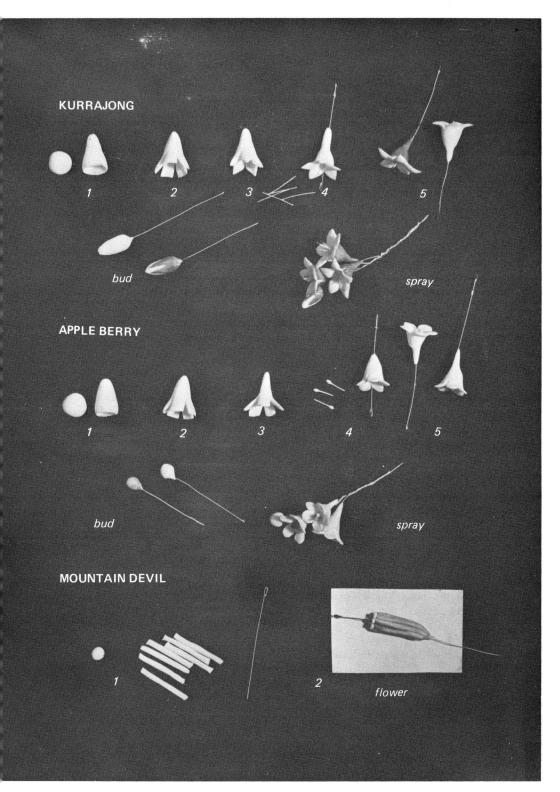

KURRAJONG

1   2   3   4   5

bud   *spray*

APPLE BERRY

1   2   3   4   5

bud   *spray*

MOUNTAIN DEVIL

1   2   *flower*

81

2. Using the pointed end of modelling stick hollow finely and make five tiny cuts to form five petals. Open out with thumb.

3. Cut each petal to a point, and press with thumb and forefinger.

4. Insert wire down through the centre, firm with fingers and taper to a fine point, cutting away any surplus paste if necessary. When dry paint burgundy red, leaving top part white and a touch of green at the base.

Bud. Mould bud shape, refer diagram, and when dry, paint as for flower.
Twist several buds and flowers close together to form a spray. Bend flower heads slightly forward.

COMMON HEATH

The Common Heath is the State flower of Victoria. Make as for Native Fuchsia. The flowers, about half the length, are white, red or delicate pink. Refer diagram.

ERIOSTEMON

The eriostemon is a dainty five-petalled flower belonging to the Boronia family. Mainly white, the backs of the petals are soft pink, while tiny white stamens tipped in red form a cluster in the centre. It lends itself to arrangements on wedding cakes or special occasion cakes where pink has been introduced. It is also lovely when used in an arrangement of wildflowers, having a softening effect when arranging among the brightly colored Christmas bells, waratah and Christmas bush.

1 and 2. As for bouvardia.

3. Cut into five equal parts, taking cuts well down into the centre.

4. Cut each petal to shape, slightly curving the sides about ⅔ of the way. "Thin" petals, insert wire down through the flower, firm at base with fingers and cut away surplus paste. Curve one or two petals slightly to give a softening look to the flower.

5. The stamens in this flower are so dainty, I use only the stem part of the stamen. Cut about five pieces of white stamen about 7 mm (⅜ inch), and holding flower at base, using tweezers, insert stamen pieces into the centre upon completion of the flower.
When dry, paint just a touch of pink on the backs of the petals and tip stamens red with a fine brush.

Bud. Mould tiny piece of paste to form a pointed bud, wire and when dry, tip bud a deep pink and paint a tiny calyx around base.
Twist several buds and flowers to form a spray.

CHRISTMAS BUSH

This dainty flower gives an added touch of color in an arrangement of Australian wildflowers.

More wildflowers. Instructions for waratah and native fuchsia, page 80.

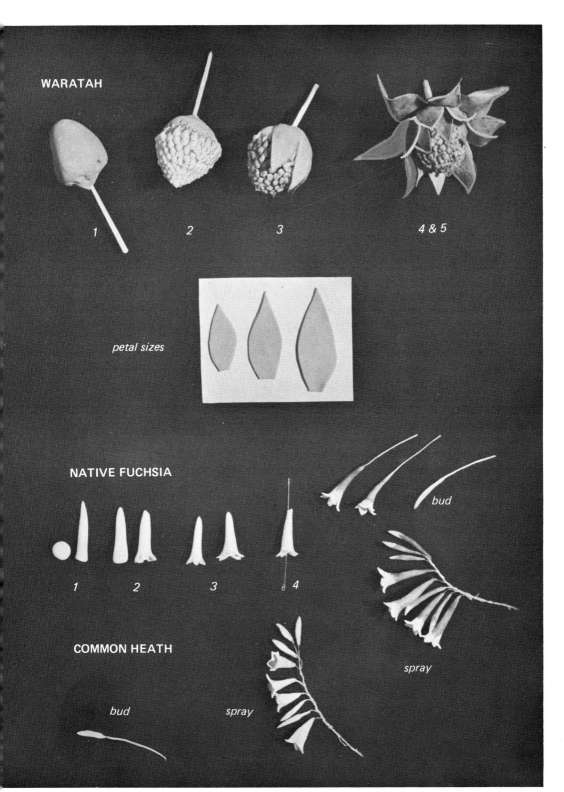

WARATAH

1 2 3 4 & 5

petal sizes

NATIVE FUCHSIA

1 2 3 4

bud

spray

COMMON HEATH

bud spray spray

Make exactly as for eriostemon. Stamens need not be added as they are so small. When painting the flower add a touch of yellow into the centre with brush, which is very effective.

To paint flowers.
When dry, paint flowers, blending your colors. If you look closely at Christmas bush when in flower, you will notice the color varies from bright scarlet inside and outside on some flowers, while others are shades of pink and cream on outside. The color is rather unusual, and you should experiment with a real flower beside you if possible to obtain the required shade.

Buds. The buds are not much bigger than a pin head and it is really not necessary to include buds in a spray. However, if required, pipe a tiny dot of pale green royal icing on end of wire.
Christmas bush flowers vary in the number of petals from four to six, but the accepted number is five petals.

Leaf. Follow diagram.

SCOTCH THISTLE

I have been asked many times "How do you make Scotch thistle?", and realised it was a flower which would have certain appeal, so have included it in this book. It is quite simple to make and can be arranged to look very attractive.

1. Stamen stems are used to make the flower, and like bottle-brush, it may be tinted with a brush after the flower has set.

2. Mould a marble-sized piece of paste in pale green into a ball, insert wire and firm at base. Hold top firmly and immediately insert about four dozen stamen pieces about 2 cm (¾ inch) into the top. Leave to completely set.

3. Using a No. 0 or 00 tube and green royal icing, pipe a squeeze and pull over the base until it is completely covered. It is just a dot pulled off to a point. When dry, paint base a deeper shade of green, being careful not to soften royal icing. Leave to completely dry, if necessary trim top with scissors, and color mauve. The completed flower looks very effective. A leaf may be moulded, wired, and twisted behind a flower.

HEATHER

This dainty flower will naturally be teamed with Scotch thistle. It is really very simple and quick to make, but you must be able to handle the tiniest piece of paste, as the flowers are very small. First cut some fuse wire into lengths 3.5 cm (about 1¼ inches) and put a tiny hook on the end.

1. Mould a very tiny piece of paste, just as if it were a bud, insert wire, flatten top with finger and place the point of your modelling stick into the centre. Leave to dry. Hold bud with fingers while you do it or you will knock it off the wire. It will take about 15 tiny flowers

Top: Assembly stages for eriostemon. Bottom: Christmas bush showing leaf pattern and wired leaf. Instructions, page 82.

84

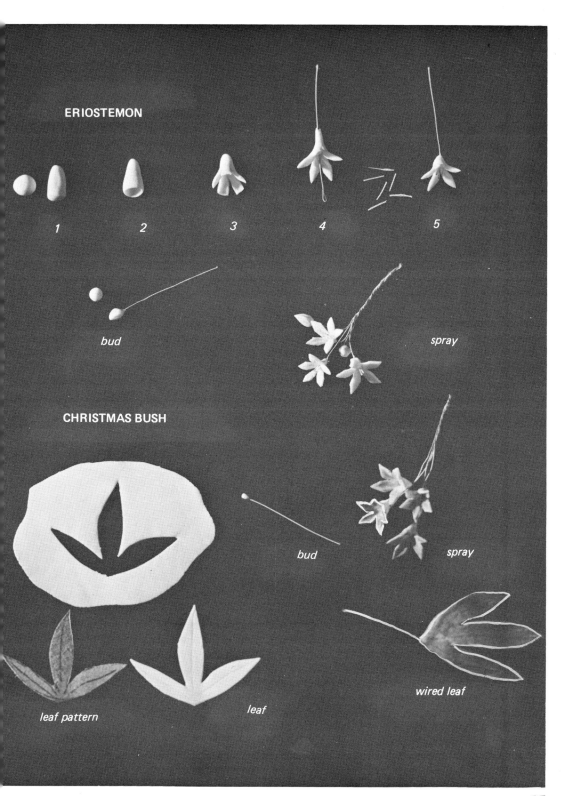

ERIOSTEMON

1

2

3

4

5

bud

spray

CHRISTMAS BUSH

bud

spray

leaf pattern

leaf

wired leaf

to make a spray. Make several tiny leaves to give a natural appearance to the spray. They are just tiny spikes and there is no need to color the paste. Tiniest pieces of paste are placed on wire, pointed and left to dry.

To assemble. When completely dry, twist flowers one after another and very close together, adding a leaf here and there. With tweezers bend flower heads slightly. You will find it easier to paint when assembled. Hold by stem and paint flowers with a mixture of mauve and burgundy red, in a pastel shade.

BOTTLEBRUSH

Perhaps you have never thought of making Bottlebrush. It is really quite simple to make, and is a lovely addition to a wildflower arrangement.

1. If you haven't any stamens with red stems, then you will have to color them with food coloring. These form the flower head and are about 2 cm (¾ inch). You might find it easier to touch up with a brush when flower is set.

2. To make the base of the flower, roll a pea-sized piece of pale green modelling paste between fingers, flatten top and with pointed end of modelling stick, hollow slightly. Do not hollow finely as there must be some thickness around the edge to allow for stamens. Insert wire down through the centre and firm at base with fingers.

3. Holding the base gently but firmly between the thumb and forefinger, using tweezers, insert stamen pieces around the rim. It will take about two dozen to complete the flower. Insert one slightly longer into the centre. You will require six to eight flowers to form one stem. When completely dry, paint base of flower a soft green.

Buds. Mould buds to shape as shown, insert wire, and when dry, paint green with a touch of red at the tip.

Twist flowers one after the other in a spiral effect, adding several buds at the base. Small wired leaves may be added if desired to complete the flower. Roll small pieces of pale green modelling paste between fingers, insert wire, flatten and point with fingers, and when dry, paint.

PINK BORONIA

This particular boronia has four tiny petals and is a lovely shade of deep pink. It adds to the appearance of a wildflower arrangement.

1. Using a very small piece of paste, roll between fingers to form a cone shape and hollow finely.

2. Cut to form four tiny petals.

3. Cut each petal to a point.

4. Insert wire down through the centre, firm at base and cut away

Two designs for a Scottish decor: Scotch thistle and heather. Instructions, page 84. A colorful Australian native is shown on the bottom row: Bottlebrush flower, bud, leaf, and assembled spray.

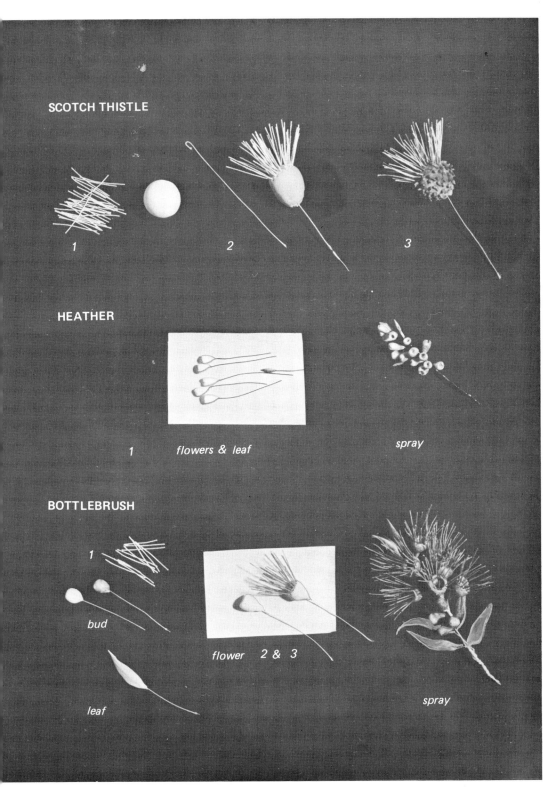

SCOTCH THISTLE

1

2

3

HEATHER

1   *flowers & leaf*   *spray*

BOTTLEBRUSH

1

bud

flower   *2 & 3*

leaf

spray

any surplus paste. Insert four pieces of cut stamen or when painting flower brush a touch of lemon in the centre.

Buds are tiny, plump and pointed.

Paint flowers using burgundy red and a touch of mauve. Twist several flowers and buds to form a spray and a tiny wired leaf for added realism. Tip stamens yellow.

Leaf. Roll the tiniest piece of paste between fingers, insert wire, flatten between thumb and finger and point. Paint when dry, and alternate with a flower when assembling.

NATIVE ROSE

This attractive four-petalled wildflower is deep pink and one which will appeal to the keen decorator. Three buds and several flowers form a "head" of flowers, and several tiny leaves are spiralled down the stem immediately behind the flowers.

1 to 4. As for pink boronia. After inserting wire, pinch each tiny petal with fingers to a point.

When dry, paint flowers a deep rose pink and add a touch of lemon in the centre. Twist flowers and buds to form a spray as shown in diagram. Now finger-shape four tiny leaves in green, and as each is made, point with fingers and attach to wire. Each leaf slightly overlaps the one before to give a spiralling effect. When set, touch up leaves in color.

BUSH BORONIA

This boronia has five petals and the cup-shaped flower is a lovely pastel shade of pink with a touch of mauve.

1 to 4. As for pink boronia. This time cut five petals, shape over rounded end of modelling stick, insert wire and add several pieces of cut stamen.

Paint flowers when dry and tip stamens yellow. A wired leaf may be added. See pink boronia. Buds are plump and pointed.

Flowers and buds may be twisted one after another to form a spray or bound with green cotton.

YELLOW BORONIA AND BROWN BORONIA

Both the yellow and brown boronia have four petals and the flowers are cup-shaped. The yellow boronia is completely yellow, the brown boronia is yellow inside, the centre and outside of the flower brown. Mould the flower in yellow and paint outside when dry.

First set a tiny piece of paste on to the end of a wire, flatten top with finger and for brown boronia, paint top brown and leave to dry.

1 to 4. As for pink boronia. After cutting four petals, cut off the corner of each petal to round the top and shape over rounded end of modelling stick to cup it. Insert tiny centre, not forgetting to lightly moisten the back, firm with fingers, cut away surplus paste and leave to dry.

Three types of boronia: Pink boronia, bush boronia and brown and yellow boronia. Native rose is also included in photograph.

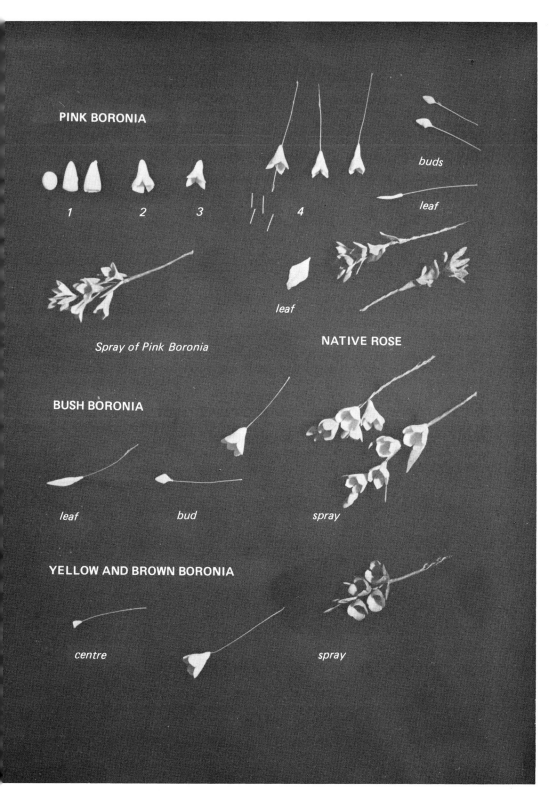

PINK BORONIA

1   2   3   4

buds

leaf

Spray of Pink Boronia

leaf

NATIVE ROSE

BUSH BORONIA

leaf   *bud*   *spray*

YELLOW AND BROWN BORONIA

centre   *spray*

Bud as pink boronia.

Twist several buds and flowers to form a spray, adding a wired leaf if desired. **Note** – Add color to top of centre only, otherwise when completing flower, the color will run. Alternatively, carefully paint on completion of flower.

AZALEA

The single azalea is not difficult to make, looks very dainty, combines well with small flowers, and may be made in several lovely shades of pink or mauve, also white. The flower is trumpet-shaped and about half way opens out into five petals. This flower would be very suitable for an all-white wedding.

With this method, royal icing is not required to assemble the flower. Before starting on the flower, take a square of alfoil about 7.5 cm (3 inches) and pleat with fingers in several places to form a cone.

1. Take a look at the diagram for the correct shape of the petals, and either finger-shape or cut out five petals, one at a time. As each one is made, finger to a nice fine edge, "flute" and fold petal lengthwise and lightly pinch down the back, or place modelling stick firmly down the centre to groove. Position the first petal.

2. Finger the next petal, lightly moisten the base only on the back and immediately position, the petal just slightly lapping the previous petal.

3. Continue until the five petals have been positioned. Using tweezers, add eight long fine-tipped stamens and one extra long stamen into a little royal icing when flower has set. Use pieces of rolled alfoil to hold stamens firm until completely dry.

Flowers may be wired and arranged singly.

Bud. Mould bud shape as shown, insert wire, and with fingers, pinch bud lengthwise in three or four places. When dry, paint a calyx around the base. The complete stamen is color of flower.

Leaves are long and oval shaped.

KARUME AZALEA

This is a miniature azalea, may be made in shades of pink or mauve. It looks lovely on a christening cake.

1. Using a small ball of modelling paste, roll between fingers and flatten top.

2. Hollow.

3. Using scissors, cut into five petals.

4. Cut each petal to a point, rounding the sides.

5. "Thin", insert wire down through the centre, cut away any surplus paste and taper down the wire.

Azalea is an ideal choice for wedding and Christmas cakes. Standard size flower is shown at top, and miniature karume azalea in lower section.

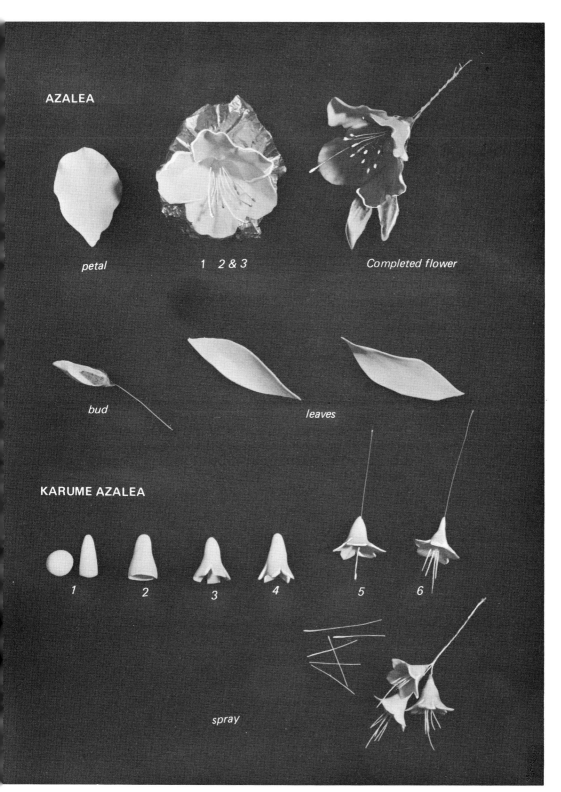

AZALEA

petal   1   2 & 3   Completed flower

bud   leaves

KARUME AZALEA

1   2   3   4   5   6

spray

6. Insert five long pieces of cut stamen and one longer piece.

To paint flower. When thoroughly dry, paint flower, tip stamens red and add a touch of green around the base.

Flowers may be added singly to an arrangement or two twisted together.

CHRISTMAS BELL

If well moulded and artistically colored, the Christmas bell is a wonderful flower to include in a wildflower spray or a Christmas decoration. If you have not been able to mould beautiful Christmas bells before, then try again.

1. Using a marble-sized piece of paste, roll between fingers to a cone about 2 cm (¾ inch) in length and flatten top with finger.

2. Pierce top with pointed end of modelling stick, then hollow with rounded end, taking it well down into the centre. Leave a slight thickness at the base to secure the wire and stamens.

3. Make six small cuts about 5 mm (¼ inch) to form six petals. Cut first in half, then each half into three.

4. Cut petals to a point, slightly rounding the sides.

5. Now "thin" bell, once again place rounded end of modelling stick into bell to ensure a nice shape.

6. Finally insert wire down through the flower, and immediately with tweezers, add six fine orange-tipped stamens into the base, just long enough to come to the top of the flower. Place flowers upside down to dry. Vary the appearance of the flower, turning some petals out, others in towards the centre.

Bud. Make buds various sizes as shown, insert wire, make several cuts over the top with scissors and leave to dry. When dry, paint as for bells, brushing a little green towards the tip.

To paint flowers. Beautifully painted Christmas bells can be eye-catching. See page 93. Avoid applying color in distinct bands of scarlet, orange and yellow, which is a common fault applying not only to beginners. Treat each flower individually, after all, every flower is not exactly the same. Vary the shading and so add interest to the spray when completed. Use two brushes either a No. 3 or a No. 5 so that you are not constantly washing brushes to change color. First brush both inside and outside the bell with a mixture of yellow and orange. While still wet, brush scarlet on the outside of the flower. Start at the bottom and brush color through towards the tip, tapering into the yellow.

When dry, assemble into sprays, two or three buds and four or five flowers will make a nice spray. Bind stems with green cotton.

IXIA

Perhaps you have never considered this flower. Ixias are simple to

Four small flowers to include in arrangements. Top: Christmas bell flower, buds, and spray. Middle row: Ixia and freesia. Bottom: Weigela, showing back of flower at left. Instructions, page 94.

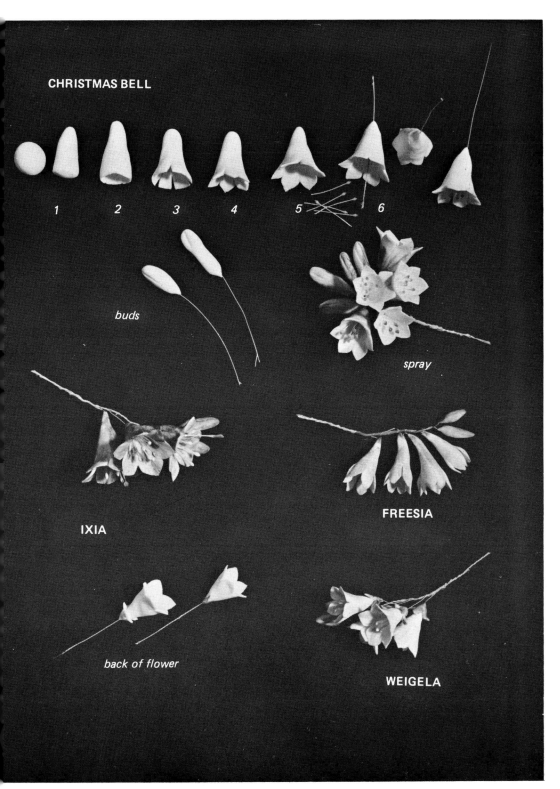

CHRISTMAS BELL

1   2   3   4   5   6

buds

spray

IXIA

FREESIA

back of flower

WEIGELA

93

make. Some of the colors are quite beautiful and make lovely sprays for cake decoration. They combine well in an arrangement of mixed flowers, particularly geraniums.

1 to 6. Make exactly as for Christmas bell. The flowers are trumpet-shaped like the freesia, so when hollowing, taper the flower towards the base. After inserting wire, with tweezers, add five yellow fine-tipped stamens and one green-tipped stamen slightly longer.

Bud. Mould bud shape and wire. When dry, paint bud adding a touch of green around base.

The colors which can be used for this flower are so varied, you would need to refer to a good garden book. They are well worth the effort to make.

Twist several flowers and buds to make a spray.

FREESIA

Freesias make a really striking arrangement on a wedding cake, particularly in shades of cream and yellow. Small white flowers such as snowdrops and hyacinths would combine well with this flower.

1 to 6. As for Christmas bell. The flowers are more trumpet-shaped, so when hollowing, make the flower tapering towards the base. Add three white-tipped stamens.

Closed flower. Make as for flower only smaller. After inserting wire, close petals over with fingers and leave to dry.

Bud. Mould bud shape, insert wire and when dry, paint pastel green with a touch of color on the tip.

There are many colors from which to choose when you paint this flower – cream, yellow, orange, pink, blue, mauve and white. Obtain a good photograph to get the correct color.

Twist two buds, one closed flower and two or three flowers to make a spray. With tweezers, bend flower heads slightly.

WEIGELA

If you have already made Christmas bells, and maybe freesias or ixias, then you will have no trouble making the weigela. This lovely flower has splashes of color from pale pink to almost red, and can be assembled to make an attractive arrangement.

1 to 6. Make as for Christmas bell, this time cutting into five petals, adding five white-tipped stamens and one longer. Leave to dry.

Either paint on a calyx around base of flower or mould a calyx. Roll on a tiny piece of pale green paste and cut into a five pointed calyx. Moisten base of flower, open calyx point with thumb, and insert into calyx. Firm and leave to dry.

Closed flower. As for freesia.

Bud. Mould bud shape wire, and paint when dry.

Top: Tiger lily flower, petal, and stamens. Lower half: Hibiscus, showing separate petal sizes for a small and large flower, centrepiece, and leaf. Instructions, page 96.

94

TIGER LILY

1   2 & 3

4   flower

HIBISCUS

2 & 3

small   flower

1

large   flower

leaf

TIGER LILY

This flower can look very attractive for a cake decoration providing petals are shaped and allowed to dry with plenty of curl. It is naturally a large flower, so must be scaled down to make it suitable. There are several lovely shades from which to choose, such as cream, yellow, pink and white. The flower has six long oval petals arranged in two sets of three, with six stamens and an anther.

This flower can also be made without the use of royal icing to assemble. Take a square of alfoil about 9 cm (3½ inches), pleat with fingers to form a cone, and roll back the edge to take the curved petals. Place in an egg cup so curved petals will not be damaged.

1. Roll out modelling paste finely and cut six petals, about 5 cm (2 inches) long and 2 cm (¾ inch) wide, one at a time.

2. As each petal is cut out, finger lightly and using modelling stick go around edge firmly with a roll and press motion. It will make the petals curly. Then "flute" the petal and lightly groove down the centre with modelling stick and place in cupped alfoil. Position the first petal, and as each petal is attached, moisten the back of the base of petal only. The second row of three petals alternates with the first row, and when attaching the second row, make sure the petals are firmly positioned. Leave to completely dry and set. **Note** – only a touch of moisture is required to attach petals. If necessary, place a piece of rolled alfoil beneath petals in the second row.

3. Make the six stamens. If you are a beginner, use bought stamens. You will need the full length of the stamen, 5 cm (2 inches) – the stem only. Mould the tiniest piece of paste to shape and place on end of stamen. A tiny round piece is set for the anther. See diagram.

4. Squeeze just a little royal icing into the base of flower to attach stamens. Support with pieces of rolled alfoil until dry.

Painting the flower. Use either a real flower or a good photograph when painting the flower. The tiger lily petals may be directly spotted in color with a paint brush or using a No. 00 tube, pipe dots, allow to dry, then paint.

Place flower upside down in a cup to attach a wired calyx.

Note – petals may be shaped on alfoil strips and allowed to dry in the same way as for water-lily. When completely dry, squeeze a little royal icing into cupped alfoil and assemble flower.

HIBISCUS

The hibiscus can be made in several attractive colors suitable for cake decoration, cream, yellow, pink and apricot shades. This is a large flower and patterns for two sizes are given. It is a five petalled flower, the large flower having a stamen about 8 cm (3 inches) and the small flower 5 cm (2 inches).

Once again the flower may be made without the use of royal icing to

Frangipani, a favorite for wedding cakes. This design may be either assembled and left on alfoil, or wired to give extra height to an arrangement.
Instructions, page 98.

FRANGIPANI

1

2

B
A
C
A

3

4

5

bud

small flower

assemble it, except to attach the stamen. Before starting on the flower, take a square of alfoil large enough to assemble the flower, pleat with fingers to form a cone, and roll back the edge to take the curved petals.

1. First make the stamen. Using a small ball of paste, roll with fingers on board to the length required, thinner towards the top, tapering slightly thicker towards the base. Into the tip, insert five stamens about 1 cm (½ inch), see diagram. Leave to completely dry. When dry, using either a No. 000 or No. 00 tube, pipe dots pulling each one to a point at the top of the stamen for about a quarter of the length. While still wet, sprinkle with lemon jelly crystals. Open stamens and leave to dry.

2. Cut five petals, one at a time. The flower is made exactly the same as azalea. This time after each one is cut, finger around the edge, "vein" the petal lengthways, and then, using modelling stick, work around the petal with a roll and press motion firmly. It will make the petal edges curly. Then "flute" and place into cupped alfoil. As each petal is made lightly moisten the back of the petal to the base only and position, slightly overlapping the previous petal. When all five petals have been positioned, leave to completely dry.

3. The flower may be painted next, allowed to dry and then the stamen set into position. Stamen is painted the color of the flower, deeper at the base and lighter towards the top. Set stamen with a little royal icing, holding in an upright position with several pieces of rolled alfoil until completely dry.
To wire flower, place carefully upside down on a cup, attach calyx and leave to dry. Handle flower carefully.

FRANGIPANI

This truly beautiful flower is not only a firm favorite for wedding cakes, but also for special occasion cakes, the touch of yellow giving a lovely fresh look to the cake. White hyacinths, snowdrops or lily-of-the-valley team well with this flower, and for a dainty appearance to the spray, make ribbon loops using only a selvedge of the ribbon.
This flower is perhaps one of the most difficult to perfect and will require a lot of practice, but with patience and perseverance, you will soon master the technique. Make the petals separately, allowing them to dry and then assembling with royal icing is completely dispensed with if you use this method.
Note. To make, use either a pattern or cut a cutter from shim brass. Buy a small sheet of .005 shim brass and using scissors, cut out a pattern and join with Araldite.
Before starting the flower, cut some alfoil squares about 6 cm (2¼ inches), make a hole in the centre sufficiently large enough to take the base of the flower. You will find this very helpful when completing its final stages.

1. Roll sufficient modelling paste finely to cut five petals at the one time. As you pick up each petal to attach, run fingers lightly around the edge to ensure fine edges.

2. Take a look at diagram 2, and using paint brush, moisten petal from A to B along edge only. Take your second petal and lap A to C directly on top of A to B and gently but firmly press into position. Be very careful at that point not to apply too much moisture, otherwise you will find the moisture will spread. The edge of the petal to be curled will become stuck and you will not be able to curl it. At the same time, make sure when adding each petal it is firmly attached, otherwise when you pick up your petals to join the flower, it will fall apart.

3. Continue until all petals have been positioned, not forgetting to moisten along the edge of the last petal. Now pick up petals, and with the back of the flower facing you, lap right side over left and firmly press to join flower. Make sure you lap correctly, otherwise you will break the spiral effect in the centre. Twist base with fingers.

4. Place base of flower through the hole in alfoil, and using the modelling stick (pointed end) work down behind the right hand side of each petal, curling it, and at the same time, place a piece of rolled alfoil behind each petal to hold in position. Be careful not to embed it in the paste, otherwise you will not be able to remove it when flower sets. I have found this an excellent idea to help beginners. Now place the flower in the neck of a small medicine bottle to dry. If an open flower is required, with fingers carefully open petals outwards. If a more closed flower is required, cup alfoil around petals to the desired position. To make a small flower for the tip of a spray, simply cut smaller petals. Remove alfoil with tweezers.

5. The frangipani flower may be wired. It will give you not only height to your arrangement and enable you to arrange small sprays of flowers with ease, but also dispenses with the use of royal icing to attach flowers to cake. Hollow a small ball of green paste just large enough to take the base of the flower. Insert wire, moisten lightly inside and insert base of flower, firm with fingers and place flower upside down to dry. If you find you need a heavier wire to support the flower, take a length of your heavy wire, about 10 cm (4 inches), double it, then twist and use.
Every flower does not require wiring. In this case, instead of attaching flower to cake with royal icing, note where the flower is to be placed, then with a knitting needle, pierce the icing and work a hole just large enough to take the base of the flower. Squeeze in a little royal icing and position flower.

Bud. Using a small piece of paste, mould bud to shape as shown in diagram, insert wire up through the base, firm and leave to dry. When dry, paint all over in soft yellow, add a touch of pink and a little green. Allow to dry, in case color runs, and with fine brush, mark an S shape with brown food coloring to accentuate the petals, then leave to dry.

Painting the frangipani. Painting the frangipani must be done artistically, otherwise a beautifully made flower will be ruined. Flowers must be completely dry before painting. First brush over top of petals with a wet brush (do not apply too much moisture). Now add a spot of yellow into the base of the flower and brush the color upwards tapering off. Remember every flower is different – some flowers have a soft touch of pink on the outside of the petals. DO NOT end color in a distinct band.

There is also the pink frangipani, perhaps not so popular, but equally as lovely. For this unusual coloring, refer to a real flower or a good flower book.

Leaf. Use moulded rose leaves, the frangipani leaf is large and not suitable for cake decoration.

I have given you instructions for making the frangipani in detail to enable you to make a perfect flower, and if you follow the instructions, you cannot go wrong. Here are a few more simple hints if you are a beginner.

(a) If you find your flowers are a little thick, don't worry, you can't expect perfection the first time. Practice will correct the fault.

(b) If you find petals are cracking when you curl them, it could mean one of two things. You are not working quickly enough and your paste is drying before you have completed the flower, or your paste is too firm when you have started to make the flower. Try using a softer consistency, this will give you more time to work the flower.

ORCHID

Orchids are very popular for a wedding or anniversary cake and may be made in many lovely colors. Refer to a good flower book to obtain the correct coloring and shaping of petals. There are many varieties of orchids, this particular one is a cymbidium.

Try to mould the petals as finely as possible and place in a natural position to set. Finger each petal after cutting to take away the "cut out" appearance, and shape with a tip turned back or an edge curled. As each petal is made, pinch along the back of the petal at the tip with the thumb and forefinger. When adding ribbon to the arrangement, cut just a selvedge and loop, it will give a softening look to the spray.

Before you start the flower, fold some strips of alfoil in the same way as you did for water-lily. Don't forget to have the strips nice and smooth. Imagine the strip is the petal, curve it in the position the petal will set, then rest the petal on it to set.

1. The orchid has five petals, a tongue and a fluted lip. Roll out modelling paste finely either in off-white or a pastel color of your choice, and cut two side front petals, shape and place on alfoil strip to dry. **Note.** When placing them and the two side back petals to dry, set in opposite positions to make a pair.

2. Cut out two side back petals, finger and pinch near tip. Place on alfoil strip in the position you want them to set.

3. Cut out centre back petal and treat in the same manner.

Stages of assembly for the beautiful cymbidium orchid. Work from a real flower or photograph, if possible, to capture the delicate tones.

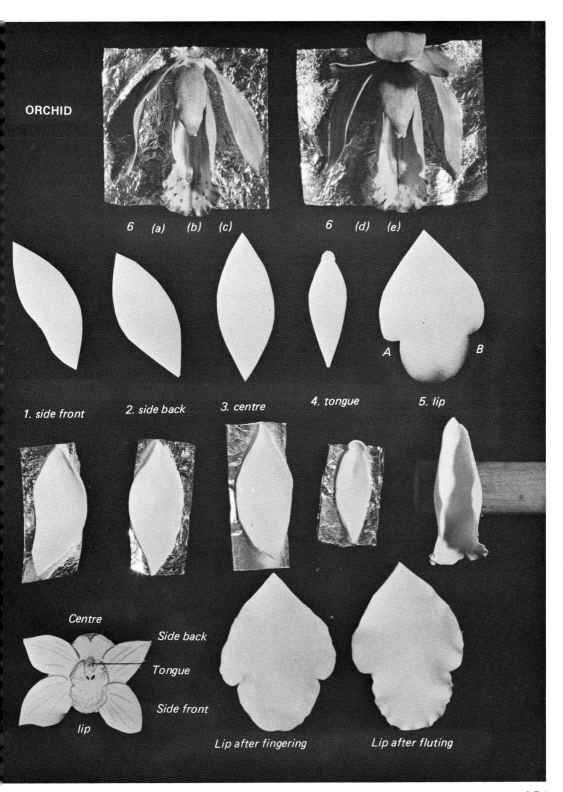

ORCHID

6   (a)   (b)   (c)   6   (d)   (e)

A   B

1. side front   2. side back   3. centre   4. tongue   5. lip

Centre

Side back

Tongue

Side front

lip

Lip after fingering   Lip after fluting

4. The tongue is slightly hooded and fleshy in appearance, so there is no need to roll paste finely. Cut tongue, roll lengthwise around meat skewer and shape top over rounded end of modelling stick. Set aside curved to dry.

5. The lip is the hardest part to make, so use a softer consistency of paste to give you time to shape the petal. Roll out paste finely leaving a slight thickness from A to B. Cut out, pick up petal and first finger around the edge from A to B. That will make the fluted lip larger, see diagram. Then with modelling stick, work around the edge with a roll and press motion to make it wavy. Finally "flute" to give extra curl. Place over the cushion part of the thumb to cup it, and shape as shown over a piece of dowel (about 2 cm, ¾ inch) to dry. When dry with a No. 3 tube, pipe two lines close together from the back of the petal down the centre to the fluted lip. Now pipe a second row on top of the first row. Using a damp brush, lightly flatten and leave to dry.

Painting the flower. The petals may be painted now, left to dry and the flower assembled. The flower must be handled carefully, and petals completely dry before assembling.

6. To assemble the flower. Take a square of alfoil sufficiently large enough to assemble the flower – about 9 cm (3½ inches).

(a) Use just enough modelling paste to set the flower. With scalpel make a cut, squeeze a little royal icing into the cut, and position the fluted lip. You will find the combination of paste and royal icing will set the flower firmly. With scalpel, cut away any paste directly beneath the lip.

(b) Position tongue directly at the base of lip.

(c) The two side front petals are positioned next.

(d) Then the two side back petals.

(e) Finally the centre back petal.

Cut away any surplus paste from back of flower, and when dry, paint the same color as the flower. Pipe two dots of royal icing on the tip of the tongue. If necessary, support the two back petals until flower has set.

WATER-LILY

Water-lilies may be made in some lovely pastel colors, such as cream, yellow, pink and mauve. They can make an attractive arrangement on a christening cake, but must be finely moulded and correctly shaped.

Before you start to make the flower, cut a length of alfoil and fold it lengthways three times, making it just wide enough for the width of the petal, about 2.5 cm (1 inch). Now cut this strip long enough to shape the petal, about 5 cm (2 inches). You will need to cut three rows of petals, nine petals in each row. Make extra petals to allow for breakages, and when assembling, use sufficient petals to give you an attractive flower. The outside petals turn outwards, so curve the strips to give you the shape. Don't make them any longer than 4 cm (1½ inches) and about 2 cm (¾ inch) wide. There is very little difference in the size of the next two rows of petals, just make

Stages of assembly for moulding the exotic water-lily. Alfoil is used in shaping the petals.

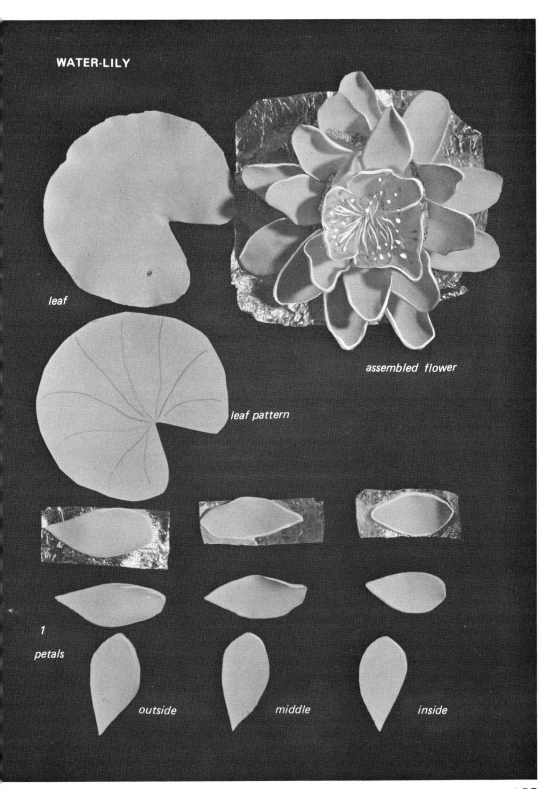

WATER-LILY

leaf

assembled flower

leaf pattern

1
petals

outside

middle

inside

103

them slightly smaller. These rows turn up around the stamens, so curve the strip accordingly. **Note.** Smooth alfoil strips with fingers. Try to cut your petals freehand, otherwise use a pattern. They don't have to be exactly the same, and don't shape petals over dowel or set in a patty tin. That makes for a most unnatural and unattractive flower.

This flower must be handled carefully, so I would advise beginners to mould in a pastel color. You will find it easier to paint later.

1. Take a look at the diagram for the shape of the petal. Roll out paste finely and cut no more than two petals at a time. While working one, cover the other with a lid. Pick up a petal and lightly finger around the edge to take away the cut look and "vein" it lengthways. If you are a beginner, leave it out. It does give an extra touch of realism to the flower.

Immediately shape the petal lengthways around your smoothed meat skewer, or a pencil will do. That will curl the petal inwards and give it a natural look. It takes only a second or two. Now place the petal on a strip of alfoil which has been curved the way you want the petal to dry. When you do that, the petal will naturally unfold again, but will still have a slight curl, which is all that is required. Make your second and third rows in the same manner, making petals slightly smaller and curving the alfoil so the petals will turn upwards. Curve alfoil in slightly different positions so petals will have variation.

To assemble the flower. When petals are completely dry, take a square of alfoil just large enough to assemble the flower. Squeeze a small circle of royal icing with a No. 5 tube, and position the first row of petals. Place your fingers in the centre to hold the petals, and cup the alfoil at the corners. Squeeze a little more royal icing around the base of the first row, and position the second row of petals, alternating with the first row. Continue until all the rows are positioned. **Note.** Petals do not overlap when assembling e.g. full blown rose. Arrange petals in a circle with the point to the centre. Squeeze a little royal icing into the centre, and with tweezers, insert about three dozen long yellow tipped stamens. Stamens completely fill the centre, bend first over finger and insert one at a time. Leave flower to completely dry before painting.

Leaf. Roll out paste finely in pale green, cut out leaf, pick up and finger around the edge, vein carefully with scalpel. Lie flat on alfoil to dry, curving the edge slightly. Paint with a mixture of brown, green and yellow.

Flower Sprays & Arrangements 5

1 *Camellia*

2 *Azaleas*

3 *Pansies*

Spring flow...

5 *Mock Orange Blossom*

6 *Field flowers*

1. CAMELLIA. One beautiful wired camellia, several buds and leaves with loops of pale pink ribbon would make a lovely decoration for a birthday or anniversary cake.

2. AZALEAS. Pale mauve azaleas make an attractive arrangement when mauve is required as the color scheme. Note the flowers have been wired, which dispenses with the use of royal icing and adds to the dainty appearance of the cake. If a larger spray is required, then add small flowers of your own choice.

3. PANSIES. These are an unusual flower to use in a cake decoration. I have arranged this spray simply with fern and loops of pale green ribbon. Wiring the flowers gives height to the arrangement and has far more appeal than if arranged flat on the cake. When painting pansies, first brush over the complete flower with the main color. While still wet, brush through other colors. The yellow pan-

7
Poinsettias

Gardenias

9 *English Briar Rose*

10 *Tiger Lilies*

11 *Water-lily*

sies were first brushed over in yellow, then mauve brushed out from the centre. I used burgundy red and apricot for the main color in the other pansies, with brown brushed out from the centre. There are many lovely combinations you could use, so refer to either a real flower or good flower book.

4. SPRING FLOWERS. A combination of daffodils, jonquils, daisies, violets, snowdrops and hyacinths have been used to make this lovely arrangement of spring flowers which would be most suitable·for a 21st birthday cake.

Flowers required: 3 daffodils
7 jonquils (2 partly opened)
5 daisies
6 violets   4 fern
6 snowdrops
6 hyacinths

12 Hibiscus

13 Australian Wildflowers

14 Orchids

15 Camellias

16 Fuchsias

5. MOCK ORANGE BLOSSOM. This flower is one which can be used for an all-white wedding cake.

6. FIELD FLOWERS. This is one instance where bright colors are permissible. Field flowers arranged with loops of red ribbon make an eye-catching arrangement on a birthday cake.

Flowers required: 2 poppies
5 daisies
3 wheat
4 buttercups
3 cornflowers
3 fern

7. POINSETTIAS. These flowers have been wired to make the arrangement far more attractive than if they were placed flat on the cake. It is interesting to note that one flower and a half flower have been used together with leaves and pale green looped ribbon to complete the spray, which would be suitable for a Christmas cake or a man's cake.

8. GARDENIAS. This is another spray which can be used for an all-white wedding cake. Wired gardenias combined with white hyacinths and a spray of stephanotis makes this a dainty spray which would look lovely on a one-tier wedding cake.

Flowers required: 3 gardenias
                      2 dozen small white flowers
                      2 leaves

9. ENGLISH BRIAR ROSE. An ideal arrangement for a small christening cake.

10. TIGER LILIES. Tiger lilies make an outstanding floral arrangement for a special occasion cake. Two tiger lilies have been wired and arranged with tulle, loops of ribbon and leaves to make this attractive spray.

11. WATER-LILY. A beautifully moulded water-lily in shades of mauve set on two leaves – a lovely idea for a christening cake.

12. HIBISCUS. One hibiscus beautifully painted, arranged with three leaves and loops of ribbon is all that is required to make this floral arrangement.

13. AUSTRALIAN WILDFLOWERS. An arrangement of Australian wildflowers such as this would be suitable for a welcome home, bon voyage or Christmas cake. The spray is a combination of wildflowers, the instructions for which are in this book.

14. ORCHIDS. Beautifully painted green orchids teamed with snowdrops would look lovely on a wedding or anniversary cake. Only the selvedge of ribbon has been used to add to the dainty appearance of the spray.

15. CAMELLIAS. Two small pink camellias with buds and leaves and a spray of jasmine make an attractive spray for a small cake.

16. FUCHSIAS. Single and double fuchsias in purples to pale pinks together with hyacinths, a spray of lilac and fern would make an admirable arrangement on a special occasion cake.

Flowers required: 4 single fuchsias
                      6 double fuchsias
                 18 hyacinths
                  1 spray lilac
                  4 fern

DEBUTANTE'S POSY

This lovely posy is not only suitable for a debutante's cake, but would look just as attractive on a 21st birthday cake. Posy may be removed from cake and kept as a memento.

Flowers required: 13 small roses in shades of pink
4 sprays each of blue hyacinths and forget-me-nots
6 sprays pink bouvardia
5 wired leaves

Cut a strip of tulle about 4 cm (1½ inches) and one and a half times the measurement of circumference of base. In this cake base was 10 cm (4 inches) in diameter and circumference 33 cm (13 inches). Now fold until desired size of scallop is obtained, carefully pin all thicknesses together and cut scallops. Using a needle and cotton, run a gathering thread along straight edge and leave for the time being.

Color modelling paste the main color of the flower spray – in this case it was pastel pink. Cut out a circle 10 cm (4 inches) in diameter and roll out to 0.3 cm (⅛ inch) at the edge, but thicker in towards the centre so you will have some depth to enable you to wire the flowers – say 2 cm (⅜ inch). Place on board lightly dusted with cornflour and leave in that position until posy has been completed, then allowed to dry thoroughly. Next draw gathering thread and fit around edge of base and set in position with a little royal icing. You might find it necessary to place a pin here and there around the edge to hold in position while you do it.

Now take two lengths of narrow ribbon, each about 61 cm (24 inches), in this case I have used one each of pale blue and pink. Loop as shown in photograph, securing beneath loops with a short twist of wire or cotton allowing tails to fall from the base and place in position. Place roses in position securing with a little royal icing, raising the four centre roses slightly with a little fondant. Now add flower sprays and last place leaves in position. As there is no depth of icing for securing the wired flowers, simply bend the wire near the base of the sprays and slide into fondant holding the posy. Set aside on a flat surface to thoroughly dry.

Posy may be raised from cake by placing two small roses at back of posy near top edge and securing with a little royal icing. Also, run a little around lower edge of posy where it touches the cake, and place in position. **Note.** Base may also be made from plastic fondant. It will take longer to set but will give you more time to assemble the posy.

LIFT-OFF POSY OF JASMINE AND VIOLETS

Simple to make, this lovely posy of jasmine and violets may be made well in advance, put away, then brought out when the occasion arises.

Flowers required: About 20 jasmine
24 jasmine buds
18 violets

Cut a piece of tulle about 6-7 cm (2¾ inches) and long enough to give you a slightly gathered circle. Scallop one side, gather straight edge and draw to fit around posy. End off gathering thread, and stitch looped ribbon in position.

Debutante's posy
(see page 109.)

Lift-off posy of jasmine
and violets

Wire flowers with a long stem, then assemble as though you were arranging a bunch of flowers. Wind a length of cotton around the stems to hold securely, then bind with narrow ribbon as shown in the photograph.

BOOTEES

Net bootees. These have been made by using cotton net, (tulle is not suitable) and dried over a small pair of plastic shoes. Cut a pattern to fit a pair of doll's shoes and then cut out carefully in net. Dip in net stiffener, pat lightly on a towel to absorb any surplus moisture and place on bootees, which have been lightly greased with a little butter to allow for easy removal. Slightly lap net at join and when dry, remove by easing around base with a needle. Em-

BOOTEES

back

front

pattern

1 2 3 4 5

Wedding Cake Vase
or Basket
(see p. 114).

broider with a No. 00 tube or cover with forget-me-nots and add a tiny ribbon bow to complete. It is not necessary to have a sole in the bootees. **Note** – this same idea can be used with modelling paste. Simply substitute modelling paste for tulle and roll out very finely.

Single bootee. Cut pattern, roll out modelling paste 0.3 cm (⅛) inch on a board lightly dusted with cornflour, cut out bootee cleanly and place on flat surface to dry, placing two icing tubes in position to allow for flower spray. Embroider and attach narrow ribbon around ankle securing with a little royal icing at back. Fill with any combina-

113

tion of tiny flowers. Flowers may be wired directly into cake, or alternatively, bootee placed on a plaque, filled with a little paste and wired into this.

Hand moulded bootees

1. Take two small balls of modelling paste exactly the same size so that both bootees will be the same size when completed. Leave one piece covered while you work the other. Have paste firm but soft enough to enable you to take the time to make the bootee before it starts to crack.

2. You will find the rounded end of your modelling stick very helpful when shaping the bootee. Pierce the centre and work to form the toe. Place the index finger into the opening to complete shaping.

3. Then work around the bootee as shown, using the modelling stick and your fingers to form the sides and back.

4 and 5. Make two bootees the same. Embroider and attach tiny narrow straps with a small run of royal icing.

WEDDING CAKE VASE OR BASKET

An attractive vase has been made by using the base of an egg cup and a small tin dish from a child's Christmas stocking. First, lightly cornflour inside of containers. Roll out modelling paste about 5 mm (¼ inch) thick on a board lightly dusted with cornflour, place in dish and trim around edge cleanly with a knife. Tip out to make sure icing is not sticking, replace and allow to dry thoroughly. Pack sufficient modelling paste into the base of egg cup, level off with knife, then tip onto board and leave to dry.

Using a No. 00 tube, work cornelli design over shapes as shown in diagram and when dry, join with a little royal icing, being careful to set base directly in the centre. Leave to set.

To assemble vase. Brush inside of vase with a little water so icing will adhere, and add either modelling paste or plastic icing, rounding in the centre and tapering to the edge. If using modelling paste make sure you have sufficient flowers made, as the paste will set quickly. Wire flowers into vase using tulle and loops of ribbon to soften the arrangement.

To make basket. Leave off the base and bind with narrow satin ribbon either several thicknesses of wire or a pipe cleaner to make the handle.

Cakes for 6
All Occasions

This chapter has been devoted to decorated cakes for all occasions, simple and elegant in design, with a wide variety of flowers and arrangements. The cakes in this section have been designed for clients' special requirements, and, although I have tried to use as many varieties of flowers as possible given in the exercises, it has not been possible to incorporate all. Many more have been shown in other parts of the book.

A general description of each cake has been given, but I think what is even more important, I have clearly indicated the number of flowers required for each arrangement, which I know every cake decorator, the beginner or the more experienced, will welcome. I cannot count the number of times I have been asked '''How many flowers will I need to make for a two-tier wedding cake, birthday cake'' or similar. This of course is to be taken only as a general guide, as no two decorators will make and arrange flowers in the same way. I do know from many years as a cake-decorating teacher, a great number of pupils, although sufficiently equipped with knowledge, after taking lessons, are still unable to create and cannot ''think up ideas''. With this in mind, I have kept the cakes simple in design with no elaborate pipe work which you would find beyond your capabilities.

I know all decorators will derive a great deal of pleasure in looking through this section, beginners will be helped enormously, and the more experienced decorators will probably form their own ideas.

VIOLETS

The unusual arrangement of this three-tier round wedding cake displays mauve violets and white violets, with just a sprinkling of white hyacinths in dainty sprays. The two lower tiers have been "stacked", adapted from the American version of a wedding cake and the top and middle tiers have been separated by pillars.

Extension has been used on the bottom tier only, while interlacing loops piped with a No. 00 tube drop from a scallop piped with a No. 3 tube on the two top tiers. Lace has been applied to the sides of the cakes in deep scallops and finished with a ribbon bow on the points. Dainty embroidered sprays have been piped freehand.

Flowers required:

Bottom tier – each of the three sprays

            16 violets some mauve and some white

            6 white hyacinths

Middle tier – each of the three sprays

            10 violets

            5 white hyacinths

Top tier   2 doz. violets

            9 white hyacinths

ROSES AND ORANGE BLOSSOM

This cream-colored cake featuring softly shaded apricot roses, orange blossom and hyacinths is particularly suited for a second wedding.

Devoid of extension, the sides of the cake are softly scalloped with lace, crimper work, let-in ribbon and dainty sprays of embroidery.

Flowers required: 3 roses

                  5 orange blossom

                  4 sprays hyacinths

                  3 fern

CHRISTENING CAKE FEATURING BABY'S LAYETTE

This beautiful christening cake won two blue ribbon awards, and features a baby's layette. Dainty sprays of pink rosebuds, snowdrops and forget-me-nots set off the softly embroidered tulle robe and bonnet. Frock alone may be used on a smaller cake or perhaps the bonnet with the bootees.

Rounded extension built out in pink, topped with a lace edging and banded by narrow pink ribbon forms the base design, while the top edge of cake is softly scalloped. Three lambs on two sides of the cake are flooded and tipped in color when dry, with a touch of grass and scattered forget-me-nots in pink and blue. A pair of moulded bootees daintily embroidered and finished with a tiny pink bow and two little bluebirds saying "Welcome" complete the design.

Bake a 25 cm (10 inch) square cake. Cut 5.2 cm (2 inches) from one side and join to one end to make cake 30 cm x 20 cm (12 inches x 8 inches). Fill in join with fondant when packing cake.

Frock. Cut tiny yoke on the double. Cut a piece of tulle for the skirt

Three-tier round wedding cake with violets and hyacinths.

116

Roses and orange blossom (instructions page 116)

Christening cake featuring baby's layette (instructions page 116)

Frangipani and snowdrops (instructions page 121).

about 33 cm x 11.5 cm (13 inches x 4½ inches) deep. Fold in half and repeat to form 16 scallops or less if desired. Pin through all thicknesses and cut scallops, gather top edge to fit waist and sew to waist by hand. Using a No. 00 tube, embroider frock and add tiny scallops to waist to hide stitching. When placing frock on cake add two tiny bows at waist, securing with a pin, and remove before cutting the cake.

Bonnet. Cut a straight piece of tulle about 10 cm x 5 cm (about 4 inches x 2 inches). Cut scallops one side and gather other side to fit a small circle of tulle to form the back of the bonnet and stitch by hand. Embroider and attach ribbon bow.

Hand moulded bootees. See page 112.

FRANGIPANI AND SNOWDROPS

The frangipani is a lovely flower in an arrangement on a wedding cake when a touch of yellow is required, and on this two-tier cake, it has been combined with snowdrops to form the floral arrangment. Small pieces of narrow ribbon have been inserted above the slight V shaped extension with a tiny leaf design piped in between the insertion. A simple embroidered spray has been piped on the sides of each cake and on opposite corners of bottom tier.

Flowers required:

Bottom – each spray	7 flowers and 4 buds
	8 sprays snowdrops
	4 leaves
Top tier	9 flowers and 7 buds
	16 sprays snowdrops
	5 leaves

SWEET PEAS

This is a flower I am sure you probably have not seen before on a wedding cake. This "different" wedding cake iced pale lemon on gold paper, features pale mauve and apricot sweet peas with cream hyacinths.

Pretty rounded extension edged in lace and finished on the lower edge with a single scallop using a No. 00 tube provides a dainty border. A very simple embroidery design has been piped freehand on each side of the cake, and a bow attached to each corner at top of extension.

Flowers required:

Bottom tier	2 sprays mauve sweet peas
	2 sprays apricot sweet peas
	6 sprays cream hyacinths
	4 small rose leaves
Top tier	1 spray mauve and
	3 sprays apricot sweet peas
	6 to 8 sprays cream hyacinths
	3 small rose leaves

Sweet peas

The simple and elegant styling of this two-tier wedding cake will
appeal to those whose choice is a round cake. Orange blossom and
bouvardia have been teamed to form beautiful sprays, the lower one
trailing from beneath the pillars, while the top tier features a lovely
rounded posy softened with a little tulle and loops of narrow ribbon.
Rounded extension edged with lace and banded with narrow ribbon
form an attractive base. Embroidered sprays piped freehand trail
from the top edge to form deep scallops around the sides of the
cake. Piped birds have been added for a final touch.

Flowers required:

Bottom tier   About 3 doz. orange blossom
                      30 sprays bouvardia
Top tier   16 to 18 orange blossom
                      18 sprays bouvardia

Daisies and hyacinths make attractive sprays on the lower tier of this two-tier wedding cake, with a half posy arrangement on the top tier. It will give the beginner a sense of achievement because there is "no extension to worry about" and will have special appeal because of its decorated simplicity.

First pipe a No. 5 shell border around the base of the cakes and then pipe a scallop directly above with a No. 3 tube. With a No. 00 tube, pipe fine lines from a dot to every alternate scallop with a half circle of accentuated dots in between.

A simple eyelet embroidery has been piped freehand on each side of the cake. **Note** – eyelets are made with the pointed end of a fine knitting needle when the covering of the cake has set, and then outlined with a No. 00 tube.

Flowers required:

Bottom tier – each spray   9 daisies
                                   15 hyacinths

Top tier   12 daisies
                                     18 hyacinths

FOUR HEARTS COMBINATION

This beautiful wedding cake would delight any bride and would be particularly suitable for a large wedding. I have used a combination of small flowers, Cecil Brunner roses, jasmine and hyacinths for the floral arrangements, which add to the dainty simplicity of this cake. The cake features a spray on each base cake with a small spray set in the recess of each heart. A ring case made from modelling paste and surrounded with a lovely spray makes a very attractive top.

It is not necessary to have extension work on a cake to make it outstanding, as this cake clearly shows. A simple shell border has been piped around the base of each cake with a No. 5 tube. Immediately above, a C border using a No. O tube completes the base design. The lovely embroidery of lily-of-the-valley sprays has been piped with a No. OO tube freehand around the cakes. The deep scallops have been piped with a No. O tube to accentuate the design. However, the less experienced decorator will find it necessary to have some guidelines from which to work.

There are seven deep scallops (each containing six scallops) piped around each cake, starting at the top of the recess of each heart and tapering to the point of the base of each cake. A lily-of-the-valley spray has been piped into each large scallop. Graduated loops have been dropped at the point of each deep scallop and the design finished with a knot ribbon bow at the back, front and two sides of the cakes. Tiny birds tipped in silver have been added as a final touch.

Flowers required:

Each base cake	9 Cecil Brunner roses
	4 sprays jasmine (3 flowers and 4 buds to each spray)
	5 sprays white hyacinths (3 flowers to each spray)
	3 leaves
Small posies at base of each cake	2 Cecil Brunner roses
	1 spray jasmine (3 flowers and 4 buds to each spray)
	2 sprays white hyacinths (2 flowers to each spray)
Top tier	7 Cecil Brunner roses
	6 sprays jasmine (3 flowers and 4 buds to each spray)
	7 sprays white hyacinths (2 flowers to each spray.

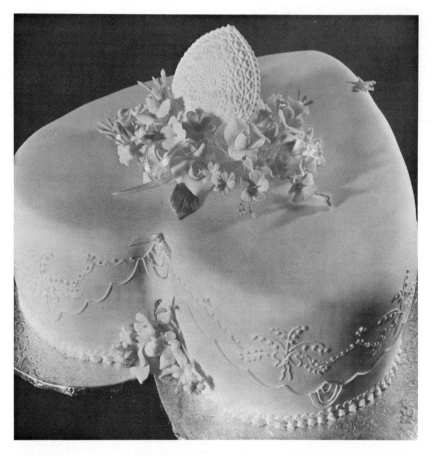

A lovely ring case made from modelling paste is far more attractive than a plastic one, and quite simple to make. It is in fact made using a plastic ring case as a mould.

Buy a ring case and separate it. Roll out firm modelling paste as finely as practicable, and place over the outside of the plastic ring case which has been well cornfloured. Carefully press over the complete surface firmly with fingers, making sure not to miss any spot, or the design will not show. Remove, place on modelling board and carefully cut around edge with scalpel. Cornflour the inside of the ring case and place inside. Tip out to make sure it is not sticking, replace and leave to set. Make the other half the same way. When dry, ease out with a needle if necessary.

When dry it is ready to assemble. Take sufficient modelling paste to fill the base to give a slightly round appearance. Lightly moisten base with a little water so it will stick, place cushion of paste into base, smooth over with fingers and taper to the edge. I have pressed the tip of a souvenir spoon around the edge to give an attractive finish. Place lid carefully into position and secure with a little royal icing. Use some support until lid sets. Finally position rings with royal icing, or they may be pressed immediately into the centre when the case is assembled. Attach a small ribbon bow where the lid is joined at the back.

FUCHSIA WEDDING CAKE

The simple styling of this wedding cake will have much appeal. Fuchsias in shades of mauve combined with white hyacinths form the attractive sprays on the lower tier, while the top tier features a posy of flowers. Sprays have been softened by the addition of tulle and loops of pale mauve ribbon.

Straight extension edged in lace forms the base border, while a dainty band of embroidery piped freehand around the sides of the cakes features mauve let-in ribbon about 1.9 cm (¾ inch) apart.

Flowers required:

Bottom tier – each spray   9 fuchsias
11 sprays hyacinths

Top tier   15 fuchsias
20 sprays hyacinths

ROUND WEDDING CAKE FEATURING ROSES

Beautiful sprays of pale pinks roses, hyacinths and forget-me-nots are the main feature on this very impressive three-tier round wedding cake.

Roses must be finely moulded, delicately painted and graduated in size.

Flowers required:

Bottom tier – each spray   5 roses and 4 buds
13 sprays hyacinths (flowers inserted singly towards tip of spray)
5 sprays forget-me-nots

Middle tier – each spray   4 roses and 4 buds, other flowers about same as bottom tier

Top tier   6 roses and 3 buds
15 sprays hyacinths
5 sprays forget-me-nots

Moulded leaves softly tinted may be added to sprays if desired.

Round wedding cake featuring roses.

HEXAGONAL ONE-TIER CAKE

This cake would be suitable as a one-tier wedding cake or perhaps
an anniversary cake, and features roses and orange blossom.
Notice this time the orange blossom has been made the "easy" way.
Simple rounded extension, lace and ribbon with dainty sprays of
embroidery make this cake one of special appeal.
Flowers required:

        6 full blown roses
     10 sprays of orange blossom
      8 sets leaves

130

21st FOR PAMELA

This pretty pale pink cake features sweet peas and rosebuds. Border has been piped with a No. 5 tube. Side treatment to this cake is an outline of lace forming large scallops above which accentuated dots have been piped. A narrow band of ribbon placed around the top edge of cake has been secured in front with two bows.
Flowers required:

        3 sprays sweet peas
        8 rosebuds
        3 fern

OBLONG 21st FOR JUDY

Sweet peas with violets and primula have been arranged in an unusual way for this 21st decoration.

Once again the appearance of this cake is simple yet elegant, extension forming the base border with the addition of ribbon and a touch of embroidery on the sides of the cake completing the design.

Bake cake in a 30 cm x 20 cm (12 inches x 8 inches) tin or use a 25 cm (10 inch) square cake and cut off 5 cm (2 inches) from one side of the cake and join at one end using a little fondant. Brush join first with egg white.

Flowers required:

Large spray – 3 sprays sweet peas
                     12 violets
                      8 primula
                      4 fern
Small spray – 7 primula
                     3 violets
                     3 fern

PHILIP AND ROBYN

Beginners will appreciate the simple styling of this white engagement cake, featuring a posy of spring flowers to celebrate the occasion.

Flowers required: 5 mauve double fuchsias
3 cream jonquils
6 sprays pale mauve hyacinths
4 violets
4 sprays cream bouvardia
2 sprays white primula
4 fern

Daisies and hyacinths are a lovely combination to delight any spring
bride.

Embroidered horseshoe and simple spray adorn each side of the
cake linked by narrow ribbon.

Flowers required:

Bottom tier   12 daisies (each spray)
                     9 sprays hyacinths

Top tier   18 daisies
                     6 sprays hyacinths around base of posy
                     A few scattered singly through posy.

Note – Hexagonal cakes have been placed on gold paper to add
to the general appearance.

GOLDEN ROSES

Round cakes placed on gold paper accentuate the lovely golden roses on this two-tier wedding cake.

Extension has been outlined with a pretty lace and freehand embroidery.

Flowers required:

Bottom tier – each spray 2 full blown roses
                                 7 sprays blue hyacinths
                                 3 leaves

Top tier   2 full blown roses (wired)
                                 8 sprays blue hyacinths
                                 3 leaves

DAINTY BESS ROSES ON A DIAMOND CAKE

Dainty Bess roses combine beautifully with primula and lily-of-the-valley to make this delightful three-tier diamond wedding cake.
The only pipe work on this cake is the straight topped extension edged in lace around the base. Tiny birds tipped in silver have been added with a piped bow trailing from the beaks.
Flowers required:
Bottom tier – each spray   3 roses
                            5 sprays white primula with lemon
                                centres
                            3 sprays lily-of-the-valley
Middle tier – The same as for bottom tier, the roses and flower sprays being smaller
Top tier   4 roses
                    7 sprays primula
                    4 sprays lily-of-the-valley

136

HEXAGONAL WEDDING CAKE

Beautifully moulded roses, hyacinths and lily-of-the-valley make an
eye-catching arrangement on this hexagonal wedding cake.
Rounded extension edged in lace with softly embroidered sides
makes this cake one of elegance and simplicity.
Flowers required:

Bottom tier – each spray	2 full blown roses
	5 sprays hyacinths
	3 sprays lily-of-the-valley
Top tier	2 full blown roses
	7 sprays hyacinths
	4 sprays lily-of-the-valley

137

**FRANGIPANI
AND LILY-
OF-THE-VALLEY**

The lovely frangipani flower has been arranged with lily-of-the-valley and snowdrops for this two-tier wedding cake. Rounded extension, shown off to advantage on a hexagonal cake, has been finished on the lower with a single scallop with a No. 00 tube. Lace and narrow ribbon complete the top edge and a rounded band of embroidery outlined with a tiny scallop worked on each side of the cake.

The spray on the bottom tier trails from beneath the pillars towards the front and slightly to the sides, so the flowers are seen from all angles. A little tulle and ribbon has been added to soften the arrangements.

Flowers required:

Bottom tier   10 frangipani in various stages and 6 buds
           5 sprays lily-of-the-valley
           15 sprays snowdrops

Top tier   7 frangipani and 6 buds
           5 sprays lily-of-the-valley
           9 sprays snowdrops

PRIMULA AND ROSES

Primula, Cecil Brunner roses and hyacinths combine to make the dainty sprays on this pretty wedding cake. Straight extensions edged with lace and finished on the lower edge with two rows of accentuated dots make an attractive base design, while an all-over design has been piped over the complete cake with a No. 00 tube.

Flowers required:

Bottom tier – each spray	7 Cecil Brunner roses
	About 16 sprays of hyacinths and primula
Top tier – vase	18 Cecil Brunner roses
	About 24 sprays of hyacinths and primula

ENGAGEMENT CAKE FOR YVONNE AND BRUCE

Full-blown roses in delicate shades of pink with blue hyacinths and pale pink bouvardia form a spray on this simply styled engagement cake.

Palest blue, the cake features rounded extension finished on lower edge with a single row using a No. OO tube. Top edge is outlined with lace and banded by narrow ribbon, a tiny knot bow securing the ribbon at each corner.

Tiny scallops following the edging of lace fall softly over the corners of the cake with a small embroidered spray piped in the corners and on the sides of the cake. Two little bluebirds and names have been tipped in silver.

Flowers required: 2 full-blown roses
9 sprays pink bouvardia
8 sprays blue hyacinths
3 leaves

140

HEARTS COMBINE FOR A 21st AND ENGAGEMENT

A lovely idea for a combination 21st birthday and engagement cake
– two large hearts iced in pale blue, arranged in an unusual way with
a beautiful spray of full-blown roses and jasmine trailing across
both cakes. The design has been kept simple so as not to detract
from the spray of flowers, which is the main feature.

A scallop with a No. 3 tube has been piped around the base of both
cakes, from which tiny interlacing loops have been piped with a No.
00 tube. A small scallop follows the top edge of the cakes, then
accentuated with an edging of lace. Narrow blue ribbon around the
cakes, secured in front with a knot ribbon bow, completes the
design.

Flowers required: 3 full blown roses
                       4 rosebuds
                       7 sprays jasmine
                       4 sets leaves
                       5 jasmine flowers at base of cakes

21st FOR HEATHER

What could be more suitable for a Scots lass than Scotch thistle
and heather?
Dropped loops with a No. OO tube interlace from a scallop piped
with a No. 3 tube around the base of cake. Lace falls in scallops
around top edge of cake and sprays of heather embroidered on two
sides of cake only, linked up with narrow ribbon, have been tipped
with color when dry.
Flowers required:

        6 Scotch thistle
     11 sprays heather
      6 wired leaves

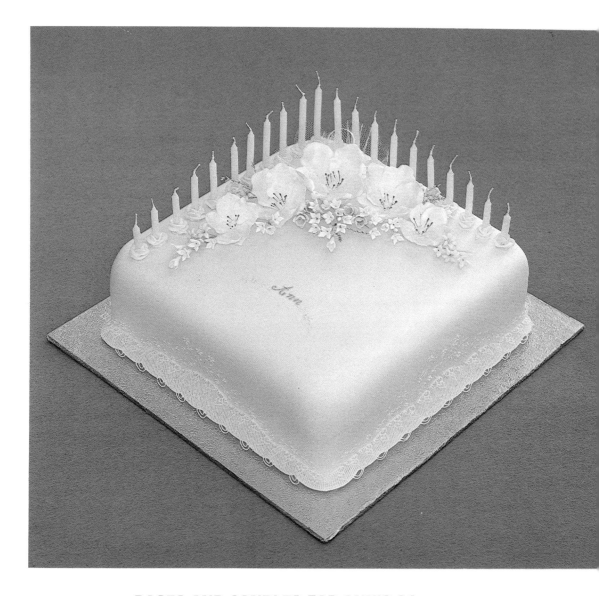

ROSES AND CANDLES FOR ANN'S 21st

Roses, bouvardia, lilac and hyacinths have been arranged to form
the attractive spray. Pretty scalloped extension and embroidery
add to the simple elegance of this cake.

Note. Candles have been cut and graduated to size, rose piped
around the base of each one and placed in position on cake after the
spray has been arranged.

Flowers required: 5 open roses
9 sprays bouvardia
4 sprays hyacinths
2 sprays lilac
3 fern

BOOTEES FOR MATTHEW

A pair of net bootees with sprays of apple blossom and forget-me-nots make a dainty decoration for a christening cake.

Pretty extension edged with lace and topped with a narrow band of blue ribbon adds to the daintiness and simplicity of this cake. "Welcome Matthew" piped with a No. OO tube and two little bluebirds have been tipped in silver.

Net bootees. See page 112.

Flowers required – each spray

        4 apple blossom

        3 sprays forget-me-nots

        2 fern

CAKE WITH A GREEK INFLUENCE

This unusual single tier wedding cake requested by an Australian girl who had spent most of her life in Greece, displays a traditional Greek design obtained from a vase I was given. It has been done in three places, around the top edge of the extension, top edge of the cake and framing the beautifully arranged spray of white hyacinths. Motifs piped between the borders around the top of the cake were also obtained from a vase.

Flowers required: You will need 12 doz. hyacinths wired into sprays and arranged artistically with the addition of tulle and loops of narrow ribbon.

LIBBY

A lovely spray of flowers transforms this beginner's cake into
something special. Medium pink roses, pink and mauve fuchsias,
eriostemon and pink and white bouvardia make an attractive spray
on this pale pink birthday cake.

Flowers required:

        3 medium roses
        3 pink and mauve fuchsias
        3 sprays eriostemon
      10 sprays bouvardia
        5 fern

BRIDAL SPRAYS

This delightful wedding cake features bridal sprays arranged on each corner of the lower tier combining lemon centred roses, hyacinths and lily-of-the-valley. A band of pretty embroidery follows the line of extension and stand-up lace beneath the pillars adds to the overall appearance of the cake.

Flowers required:

Bottom tier – each spray	3 rosebuds
	6 sprays hyacinths
	2 sprays lily-of-the-valley
Top tier	4 small medium roses
	5 rosebuds
	12 sprays lily-of-the-valley
	8 sprays hyacinths

A BASKET OF DAISIES

The simplicity of this wedding cake featuring a dainty basket of daisies, hyacinths and forget-me-nots for "something blue", will delight a beginner. There is no need for any elaborate pipe work to make a really pretty cake, and as you become more proficient, you can try your hand at something a little more involved.

It is far better to ice and decorate a wedding cake, or any cake, and be able to sit back and really feel as though you have accomplished something, than to attempt something beyond your capabilities and feel disappointed and frustrated in trying to do it.
This dainty basket is so simple to make, and may be made weeks ahead of time if you wished. See instructions wedding cake vase page 113. For the basket, simply leave off the base and add handle and ribbon bow. Bind either a pipe cleaner with ribbon, or bind several lengths of wire together with cotton and then bind with narrow ribbon. Ribbon has been cut in half to give a nice firm fit.

Design. No 5 shell border and freehand embroidery piped on sides of cake. Lace outlined in scallops around the base of cakes, and then outlined in accentuated dots. Tiny birds have been positioned on top tier only. Four dainty sprays have been arranged around each pillar.

Basket 16 small daisies
       20 hyacinths
        1 doz. forget-me-nots scattered singly through cake
Bottom tier – each spray 5 small daisies
                 5 sprays hyacinths
                 8 forget-me-nots

**DAINTY BESS
ROSES**

The unusual arrangement of flowers together with the top tier set on an angle give this two-tier square wedding cake an air of distinction. Graduated roses on the bottom tier have been arranged coming from the base up over the top of the cake with an arrangement on the opposite corner of just three roses around the pillar. Scallops of lace and a touch of embroidery are other appealing features.
Note. The two roses immediately above the three roses on the board and the rose on the corner of the cake have been "let in" to the cake covering. Note the position where the flower is to be placed and then using your scalpel carefully, cut out just sufficient icing from the cake covering to let the back of the rose be firmly positioned. Squeeze a little royal icing into the hole and leave until flowers have set before adding small flowers to arrangement.
Flowers required:

Bottom tier – large spray 8 graduated roses
about 12 sprays hyacinths
small spray 3 roses
8 sprays hyacinths
Top tier 7 roses (2 centre roses wired)
about 12 sprays hyacinths

150

AN OVAL BEAUTY

Beautifully moulded pale pink roses together with eriostemon and hyacinths adorn this lovely oval cake, a very popular shape with many brides-to-be.

A simple band of embroidery has been piped around the cake. Notice the dotted extension and "three down – one up" arrangement of the lace pieces. An oval outline of lace has been positioned beneath the pillars.

Flowers required:

Bottom tier	4 medium roses graduated
(each spray)	1 rosebud
	7 sprays pale blue hyacinths
	5 sprays eriostemon
Top tier	5 small medium roses
	9 rosebuds
	12 sprays pale blue hyacinths
	6 sprays eriostemon

Roses and hyacinths combine to make this simple three-tier wedding cake for the beginner. A No. 5 shell border has been piped around the base of the cakes. Interlacing loops have been piped directly above with a No. 00 tube. Pipe a row of loops around the cake, then starting half way between the first loop, pipe the second row. Pipe embroidered hollyhock and forget-me-not circles, then link with scallops to complete the design. Tiny birds and embroidered bows add a final touch.

Flowers required:

Bottom and middle tiers — each spray

        3 roses
        6 sprays hyacinths
        3 leaves

Top tier   4 roses
        12 sprays hyacinths
        4 leaves

152

APPLE BLOSSOM

This beautiful wedding cake would delight any bride. A lovely posy of apple blossom, with just a delicate touch of pink and lily-of-the-valley, adorns the top tier, while dainty sprays have been arranged around the four pillars on the lower tier. **Note** – only a selvedge of the ribbon has been used in the sprays, which adds to the dainty appearance.

A pretty border of scalloped extension edged in lace has been piped around the base of the cake. A very simple embroidery design following the scallops of the extension has been piped freehand with a No. 00 tube around the sides of the cake.

Flowers required:

Bottom tier – each spray 5 apple blossom (centre one wired)
4 sprays lily-of-the-valley

Top tier 15 apple blossom
12 sprays lily-of-the-valley

153

DAINTY BESS ROSES ON A DIAMOND CAKE

This beautiful design took first prize at the Sydney Royal Easter Show. The whole appearance of this three-tier cake is one of simplicity and daintiness. The slightly V shaped extension is finished on the lower edge with two lines piped close together with a No. 00 tube. Small pieces of narrow ribbon have been inserted above the extension about 20 mm (¾ inch) apart with a tiny scallop piped either side to form a band. A forget-me-not spray has been piped in between each piece of ribbon.

Fine lace has been outlined in a curved diamond shape beneath the pillars and also falls softly over the corners. An all-over design of small forget-me-not sprays with a fine dot here and there has been piped freehand over the top of the cake. Softly shaded Dainty Bess roses, just pink bouvardia and forget-me-nots form the dainty sprays which are shown to best advantage on opposite corners of the cake.

Flowers required:

Bottom and middle tiers – each spray

        3 Dainty Bess roses

        4 sprays each of bouvardia and forget-me-nots

        3 leaves

Top tier   6 Dainty Bess roses

        6 sprays each of bouvardia and forget-me-nots

        5 leaves

HEARTS AND SPRING FLOWERS

This cake will have special appeal if your choice is a heart-shaped one. The main attraction of this wedding cake is the lovely floral arrangement of roses, hyacinths, snowdrops, bouvardia and lily-of-the-valley in soft pinks and white. Flowers have been arranged on the lower tier beneath the pillars in such a way they may be seen from all angles.

Top edge of extension has been scalloped and edged in lace with a tiny scallop piped above. Dainty sprays have been embroidered at points, a narrow band of ribbon placed around top of cake and secured both back and front with a small bow.

You must be prepared to mould many tiny flowers for these sprays, but the finished cake will give you a wonderful sense of achievement and gain much admiration.

Flowers required:

Bottom tier	3 pink roses (wired) and 15 rosebuds
	22 sprays pink and white bouvardia
	24 sprays white hyacinths
	10 sprays snowdrops
	6 sprays lily-of-the-valley
Top tier	3 pink roses (wired) and 7 rosebuds
	14 sprays pink and white bouvardia
	9 sprays white hyacinths
	4 sprays snowdrops
	5 sprays lily-of-the-valley

Hearts and spring
flowers.

Here is a style suitable for a boy's 21st birthday cake, a typical example of basic pipe work and very simple for the beginner.

This 23 cm (9 inch) cake was iced in pale green on gold paper. The border has been piped with a No. 35 tube, a No. 0 for the piping either side of the narrow pale green ribbon which has been secured at each corner with a knot ribbon bow. Crimper work has been used around the top edge of the cake, and you will find it very easy to do as the edge of the cake is your guide line.

White yellow-centred daisies, cream and yellow jonquils and fern support the lemon horseshoe on "Congratulations" and pipe work piped with a No. 0 tube has been tipped in gold. The traditional 21st key has been piped with a No. 3 tube on waxed paper, allowed to dry, tipped in gold and then secured to the cake with a little royal icing. Notice the raised horseshoe in the arrangement. Simply arrange the wired flowers around the horseshoe, which not only elevate it, but hold it firmly in position, taking away the flat appearance which you would achieve if you placed it directly on to the cake.

To make the horseshoe, lightly dust the board with cornflour, roll out modelling paste as finely as practicable, place pattern in position and cleanly cut out. Round off edge with fingers and leave to dry. Add pipe work and tip in gold.

Flowers required: 6 daisies
5 jonquils
5 sprays fern

158

DEBORAH SUSAN

This lovely christening cake features karume azaleas, snowdrops and forget-me-nots arranged around a christening card with two little flooded cherubs saying "Welcome".

Soft embroidery follows the top edge of the cake with a No. 00 tube. Extension and lace form an attractive base while a narrow band of pink ribbon around the cake completes the design.

Christening card. 9.6 cm x 11.5 cm (3¾ inches x 4½ inches)

Roll out modelling paste to the desired size and use a scalpel to cut edge cleanly. Narrow pink ribbon has been attached with a little royal icing to back of card in three pieces, with just an edging of ribbon showing between the scallops.

Two little cherubs have been outlined, flooded and when dry painted with food coloring. Embroider card, outline edge with a No. 00 tube and tip in silver. Scattered forget-me-nots have a centre of glitter added with tweezers. Attach ribbon bow.

Flowers required: 7 karume azaleas
                    14 snowdrops
                   3 sprays forget-me-nots
                   3 fern

Icing 7
Recipes

MODELLING PASTE

This is the modelling paste I use and recommend. It is essential that it is made carefully and all ingredients measured accurately, otherwise you will not achieve the correct consistency, which is most important when making flowers.

Gelatine must be dissolved thoroughly, otherwise the undissolved grains will become like jelly and show up through the paste, making it useless. I stress the point, because so many beginners make that error. If insufficient gelatine is added, paste will not have sufficient elasticity, and when making petals, you will find when working the petals out finely with fingers, it will suddenly break. Too much gelatine will make the paste like a rubber ball and you won't be able to work the paste. Experience is the best teacher, and you will know by the feel of the paste when it is right. Do not overdo the glucose, remember it becomes liquid when dissolved. I would suggest you make up 250g (8 oz) only until you feel you are making it correctly. If you wish to do a lot of moulding, then make double the recipe, but be sure you double **all** the ingredients.

MODELLING PASTE RECIPE

Ingredients	Metric	Imperial
Pure sifted icing sugar	250 g	8 oz
Gelatine	2 scant teaspoons	2 scant teaspoons
Glucose	1 rounded teaspoon	1 rounded teaspoon
Water	30 ml	1 oz

Method

1. Sift pure icing sugar into a bowl.

2. Place gelatine and water into a small bowl, stand it in a saucepan containing a little water and dissolve over gentle heat. With that method you will not lose any liquid.

3. When dissolved, add glucose. The liquid should be quite clear before adding to icing sugar.

4. Make a well in the centre of icing sugar and stir in liquid with a knife.

5. Place mixture in a plastic bag and then in a container with a lid and store at room temperature. Leave to stand three to four hours before using.

ALMOND PASTE

An undercoat of almond paste gives a good base for the covering of the cake and the recipe is sufficient to cover a 20 x 20 cm (8 x 8 inch) cake. First brush over the cake with egg white before covering with almond paste.

Ingredients	Metric	Imperial
Pure icing sugar	500 g	1 lb
Ground almonds or marzipan meal	125 g	4 oz
Egg yolks	2	2
Sweet sherry	2 tablespoons	2 tablespoons
Glycerine	1 tablespoon	1 tablespoon
Sufficient lemon juice to mix to a firm dough		

Method

1. Place sieved pure icing sugar and ground almonds into a bowl. Mix well.

2. Beat egg yolks, add sherry and lemon juice and add to mixture in bowl. Knead to a firm dough, adding a little more icing sugar if too soft and a little more sherry if too firm.

3. Roll out on board lightly dusted with icing sugar, and with aid of rolling pin, place over cake which has been brushed with egg white. Roll over top and down sides with rolling pin, and rub with palms of hands lightly dusted with icing sugar to give a nice smooth surface. If using marzipan, leave one day before covering, if using almonds, leave two or three days, to prevent almond oil from seeping through and staining cover.

PLASTIC ICING

This is a very good plastic icing recipe used widely by cake decorators with assured success. It gives a lovely smooth covering and remains soft to eat. This recipe is sufficient to cover a 20 cm x 20 cm (8 inch x 8 inch) or 250 g (1/2lb) fruit cake.

Ingredients	Metric	Imperial
Pure sieved icing sugar	1000 g	2 lb
Liquid glucose	1/2 metric cup	1/2 cup
Glycerine	23 ml	3/4 oz
Gelatine	15 g	1/2 oz
Water	1/4 metric cup	1/4 cup
flavoring of own choice	several drops sufficient to flavor	

Method

1. Sieve icing sugar into a bowl.

2. Place gelatine and water into a small bowl, stand in a saucepan containing a little water (to a depth of about 4 cm (1½ inches) and dissolve over gentle heat until gelatine has been thoroughly dissolved. Using that method, you will not boil the mixture, nor will you lose any liquid in dissolving. Remove from heat.

3. Stir in glucose and glycerine (with bowl still standing in hot water) until dissolved.

4. Stir liquid into sieved icing sugar.

5. Remove from bowl and knead well until icing becomes smooth and pliable. Add coloring and flavoring and it is ready for use. Add a little extra icing sugar should the mixture be too soft. Icing may be stored in an airtight container until required at room temperature. **Note** – if you do not wish to cover the cake after making icing, don't knead in all the icing. Reserve say about a cupful and knead it in when ready to apply to cake.

PLASTIC FONDANT

An excellent fondant for covering cakes. It is particularly recommended for wedding cakes, ensuring a dazzling white smooth surface, while remaining soft to eat. This recipe is sufficient to cover an average size three-tier wedding cake or a large two-tier cake. Make at least one day before use.

Ingredients	Metric	Imperial
Group 1		
Gelatine	30 g	1 oz
Water	⅔ cup	5 fl. oz
Group 2		
Crystal sugar	500 g	1 lb
Liquid glucose	125 g	4 oz
Glycerine	30 g	1 oz
Water	⅔ cup	5 oz
Cream of tartar	1 level teaspoon	1 level teaspoon
Group 3		
Copha	125 g	4 oz
Pure icing sugar	1500 g	3 lb

Place group 1 in a bowl. To dissolve I prefer to stand bowl in a saucepan containing a little water and dissolve over gentle heat. While it is dissolving – Place group 2 in a saucepan which has been greased lightly around the top with a little copha. Place in sugar thermometer and stir over medium heat until sugar has dissolved and mixture starts to boil. Remove spoon and boil on fast heat until thermometer registers 116 deg. C (240 deg. F).
Remove from heat, allow to cool about five minutes and then stir in dissolved gelatine and flaked copha (group 3). Pour mixture into a large bowl, preferably one with a lid, and stir in icing sugar (group 3)

a cupful at a time. Clean down sides of bowl with a spatula, replace lid and leave 24 hours before use. When required, knead in extra icing sugar to obtain the required consistency.

ROYAL ICING

Royal icing is used for all pipe work and is better beaten by hand as it produces a much better piping consistency. Electrically beaten royal icing gives a false impression of consistency, and on standing, will subside because of aeration in the mixture. Use royal icing freshly beaten to achieve the best results.

Ingredients	Metric	Imperial
1 egg white		
Pure sieved icing sugar	375 g	12 oz
(amount used will depend		
on size of egg white)		
Acetic acid	2 drops	2 drops

Method. It is a good idea to have a small glass or china bowl and a small wooden spoon set aside exclusively for mixing your royal icing. Place egg white into bowl and gradually add a tablespoon of pure icing sugar at a time, beating well after each addition. Do not be tempted to add too much icing sugar too quickly, you will not achieve the same results. Continue in this manner, add acetic acid as the mixture thickens and continue beating, adding less icing sugar until mixture is thick and firm enough to hold a peak. A soft consistency is required for fine pipe work and firm for shell borders. Place in a container with a lid. Do not leave royal icing uncovered as the air will soon form a crust on top. It is not necessary to use a whole egg white, a half or even one third will make sufficient royal icing to decorate a cake.

NET STIFFENER

Only use cotton net with net stiffener when you are making something that you want to hold a shape, such as net bootees. Tulle is not suitable.

Recipe – for a small quantity.

1/4 cup pure icing sugar
1/4 cup water

Place above in a small saucepan and stir over gentle heat to dissolve. Bring to boil and simmer about three minutes. Cool and store in screw top jar.

To stiffen net, immerse pieces in stiffener with tweezers, remove and gently pat out any surplus on a towel and place over shape to set.

Cake Recipes 8

RICH WEDDING CAKE MIXTURE

This recipe I can recommend not only for that all-important cake, the wedding cake, but also for any special occasion cake as well as the Christmas cake. It is a rich moist cake, cuts beautifully and has a delicious flavor.

Recipe for 500 g (1 lb) 25 cm (10 inch) cake.

Ingredients	Metric	Imperial
Sultanas	500 g	1 lb
Currants	500 g	1 lb
Raisins	500 g	1 lb
Glace apricots or pineapple	125 g	4 oz
Prunes	250 g	8 oz
Chopped mixed peel	250 g	8 oz
Glace cherries	250 g	8 oz
Almonds – chopped	125 g	4 oz
Walnuts – chopped	125 g	4 oz
Dates	125 g	4 oz
Sherry, rum or brandy	½ metric cup	½ cup
Butter	500 g	1 lb
Brown sugar	500 g	1 lb
Eggs – large	10	10
Golden syrup or honey	1 tablespoon	1 tablespoon
Marmalade, plum or raspberry jam	1 tablespoon	1 tablespoon
Glycerine	1 tablespoon	1 tablespoon
Vanilla essence	1 teaspoon	1 teaspoon
Almond essence	1 teaspoon	1 teaspoon
Grated rind and juice of 1 lemon		
Plain flour	500 g	1 lb
Self-raising flour	125 g	4 oz
Mixed spice	2 level teaspoons	2 level teaspoons
Salt	½ level teaspoon	½ level teaspoon

¼ teaspoon bi-carbonate of soda (optional)

Method

1. Wash and dry all fruits. Cut up apricots, prunes, dates, cherries and raisins.

2. Place fruits and nuts in jar and cover. Stand several days if possible or at least overnight in spirit used.

3. Cream butter and sugar well, add eggs one at a time and mix thoroughly.

4. Add essences, glycerine, golden syrup, jam, lemon rind and juice.

5. Add sifted dry ingredients and fruit alternately to mixture until all is added.

6. Line a 25 cm (10 inch) cake tin with two sheets greaseproof paper, bringing the paper about 4 cm (1½ inches) above the tin.

7. Bake in a slow oven 140 deg. C – 150 deg. C (275 deg. F – 300 deg. F) for about 5 – 5½ hours.

8. When baked trickle 2 or 3 tablespoons of sherry, rum or brandy over cake while still hot, then wrap in several thicknesses of paper and a towel and allow to cool slowly. This slow method cooling seals in the steam and helps keep cake moist.

9. Remove from tin when cold and re-wrap until required.

HINTS FOR MAKING SUCCESSFUL FRUIT CAKES

Use a reliable, well-proportioned recipe, e.g. 250 g (½ lb) each of butter and brown sugar, 1200g (2½ lb) fruit and 315 g (10 oz) plain flour or 60 g (2 oz) self-raising flour to 250 g (8 oz) plain flour in 250 g (½ lb) cake as the basic ingredients.
Fruit cakes are referred to as 250 g (½ lb) and 500 g (1 lb) mixtures according to the quantity of butter and sugar used, **not** as the **total** weight of the cake when baked.
Bake a 125 g (¼ lb) mixture in a 15 x 15 cm (6 x 6 inch) tin.
Bake a 250 g (½ lb) mixture in a 20 x 20 cm (8 x 8 inch) tin.
Bake a 500 g (1 lb) mixture in a 25 x 25 cm (10 x 10 inch) tin.
Bake a 750 g (1½ lb) mixture in a 30 x 30 cm (12 x 12 inch) tin.
To ensure nice square corners of cake, care should be taken in lining the tin. Don't allow paper to become embedded in the mixture or when removing, the paper will pull away some of the cake.
Always wash currants, raisins and sultanas and spread evenly on trays to dry, remove pips and stalks and cut up large pieces of fruit such as dates, apricots, raisins, or others. Do not mince fruit, it cannot be separated by the cake mixture.
Do not use damp fruit.
Allow fruit and nuts to stand for several days or even longer in screw topped jar with spirits, this improves the flavor of the cake.
Have eggs and butter at room temperature, add eggs singly, beating after each addition, but do not overbeat at this tends to thin down the mixture and separate the creamed ingredients.
Eggs and butter may be beaten on mixer, then placed in large mixing bowl and mixed by hand. If mixture separates after the addition of eggs, take a little flour from the weighed quantity for the cake and blend through the mixture.
Sift spices together with flour and salt twice to ensure even blending.
If the creamed mixture is thin because of overbeating or the heat of the day, place basin in refrigerator to firm mixture before adding the weight of the fruit, and so reduce the possibility of the fruit sinking through the over-soft cake mixture.
After placing mixture in tins, spread evenly, then bump the tins several times on the table to settle the mixture.
Rich fruit cakes need not be cooked the same day as they are mixed.

They may be stored in refrigerator for several days, allowed to thaw to reach room temperature and then baked.

Bake in a slow oven for the whole cooking time. Do not put into a moderate or hot oven and then reduce heat. This practice results in the surface of the cake being baked too quickly, and the result is a hard surface and a crack on top.

When cake is removed from oven, sprinkle with two or three tablespoons brandy, sherry or rum, which is immediately absorbed into the cake. Cover with alfoil or greaseproof paper and then in several thicknesses of paper or towel.

Fruit cakes improve in keeping. Cake may be made several months before required.

Index to Flower Exercises

Page references in bold indicate photographs

172